Patricia Feinberg Stoner is a _ _ _ _
copywriter and publicist. For four years she and her husband
were accidental expatriates in the Languedoc, southern
France.

Once a fiercely dedicated Londoner, she now lives happily
with her husband and dog in the pretty West Sussex village
of Rustington, where Michael Flanders encountered a gnu
and the mobility scooter is king.

She spends much of her time writing short stories and comic
verses, many of which have been published in print and
online. Her first book, 'Paw Prints in the Butter', is a
collection of humorous poems about cats, and is sold in aid
of a local animal charity.

Patricia welcomes visitors to her Facebook page (Paw Prints
in the Butter) and to her blog: www.paw-prints-in-the-
butter.com

You may occasionally find her @perdisma.

Also by Patricia Feinberg Stoner

Paw Prints in the Butter

Patricia Feinberg Stoner

AT HOME IN THE PAYS D'OC

With illustrations by Bob Bond

Published in the UK by Fascom 2017

ISBN 978-0-9957462-0-6

Cover design by Verité CM, Worthing,
West Sussex BN12 4HJ, UK.

Cover illustration taken, with permission, from an original
painting by Florence Laiter Andersen.

Black and white drawings by Bob Bond
www.footballershappen.com

For Patrick, who made it happen,

and

For Purdey, who made us change direction,

and

For all my friends and neighbours in France who made me feel

at home in the Pays d'Oc

Contents

1

ONE:
Beginnings

'Mon dieu!' The customs officer smoothed his moustache with an agitated finger, surveying the sheaf of paperwork before him.

Three minutes earlier, he had been all Gallic chauvinism, peering disdainfully through his little window at the dusty Ford Transit sagging on its springs, at the laden trailer with here a chair leg, there a lamp shade poking out from beneath its insecurely tied tarp.

Ignoring the fact that I had spoken to him perfectly politely in French, 'Do you heff an eeenventory?' he sneered.

The man who didn't like France

When I first met my husband Patrick (also known as Himself), he announced casually, quite early on in the relationship, that he didn't like France. Curious, in a man who had travelled widely in Europe and driven a bus to India, but there it was. Well, I thought, this will not do. Either the man must go, or I'll have to change his ways. Being a woman, I opted for the latter.

After a little subtle probing, I discovered that there was one place he quite liked, one place he had visited in his wild youth and not found wanting. This place was "Capdag" – which I had never heard of. Perhaps this was a blessing. If in those early uncertain days I had found myself saddled with a man who actually liked Le Cap D'Agde, as it was then, perhaps the man would have gone after all.

It was the 1980s, an era when barrow boys made good on the stock market boom and money poured in like gin and tonic. The newly wealthy took sailing holidays in tiny craft, safely shepherded round the Med by a mother ship. They docked at the port of Cap d'Agde, a wannabe Monte Carlo, lined with burger bars and tacky souvenir shops and overpriced chandlers. Of an evening you'd see them sitting out on their pocket-handkerchief decks, drinking pina coladas and playing at being impresarios and captains of industry.

They thought themselves fine fellows; we called them the Sheep Fleet.

Still, it was France: it was a start.

6

What happened next I attribute entirely to a shared hairdresser and the power of a miniskirt. I was working at an agency in London at the time, and started going to this particular hairdresser because it was close and convenient and I liked the way the (male) stylist did my hair.

Himself started going to the same hairdresser once he discovered that not only did the (female) stylist do his hair the way he liked it, but she also wore exceedingly short skirts over exceedingly long legs.

And one day he returned from having his hair done and said, man-like, 'Oh, I saw a notice up in the hairdresser about a house to rent near Capdag. Perhaps you should make a note of the number next time you are in there and give the people a ring.'

Now in those days Patrick was still in the early stages of training, so instead of saying 'Well why the (expletive deleted) didn't you take the name and number down yourself?' I uttered that phrase every woman keeps in her armoury for occasions such as these. 'Yes, dear,' I said.

* * * * *

We began our French odyssey with a cautious toe in the water. After Himself had reluctantly agreed that we might consider France for a holiday, we decided to rent the house we had seen advertised in that hairdressing salon.

And so it was that, at the start of July 1984, we found ourselves in St Rémy des Cévennes, a busy market town in the Languedoc Roussillon.

We hated St Rémy on sight. We arrived on market day, the streets were congested, we got lost, and when we finally arrived at the house, hot, cross, weary and in need of siestas, the exceedingly fierce cleaning lady threw us out again because we were not supposed to turn up till 4 o'clock.

Things improved over the next two weeks as we came to know and love St Rémy. We never tired of exploring the tangle of the medieval quarter: winding alleys overhung by tall narrow houses, their wrought iron balconies almost touching across the street, adrip with scarlet geraniums. I would turn a corner and find myself in a tiny *place,* riotous with bougainvillea and plumbago and yet more geraniums. Outside the *épiceries* the stalls spilled out their offerings of spoiling fruit; aromas of turmeric and clove, *fromage de chèvre* and *saucisson* wafted from interiors invisible from the sunlit street.

This was life as we dreamed it should be. By the end of our fortnight's holiday we were talking tentatively about returning next year. By the middle of the following year's holiday we were saying 'When we come back next year...' And by the third consecutive year in St Rémy we were fantasising about having our own house there.

It was never meant to be more than a fantasy. Ever since we had known each other we had been making wild, improbable plans about a bolt-hole in the sun. A boat in Greece, a bar in Spain. A house in St Rémy was just another fun dream, *bien sûr.*

When we got back to England, we told the owner of our rented house that if he ever wanted to sell, we would like first refusal (looking back, we must have been mad. It was a pretty horrid house).

'Well,' said he, 'I do know someone who wants to sell a house in the area...'

Back in St Remy for the fourth time, we consulted the instructions he had given us. It was one of those typical Midi arrangements. If we went to Le Café des Arts in St. Rémy at three o'clock on a given Tuesday and asked for

8

Charlie, this person would take us to the house he was selling. Feeling rather as if we had wandered into a remake of The Third Man, we duly presented ourselves at the bar at the stated time and asked for Charlie.

Of Charlie, naturally, there was no sign. We did however get pounced on, to my horror, by a loud, mustachio'd and extremely eccentric Englishman who, improbable though it may seem, dragged us to his table with the words 'Any friend of Charlie's is a friend of mine.' As the Englishman looked like a cross between Astérix the Gaul and an unmade bed, this was hardly reassuring.

Well, since Charlie had failed to show, we obviously weren't going to be buying any houses. Or perhaps...? It was then that Himself noticed that the café we were sitting in was directly opposite an estate agency, and said, 'Well, it wouldn't hurt to go and look in the window, would it?'

This was how we came to meet the estate agent Jean-Jacques. Jean-Jacques was small and voluble with a cheerful grin and no English. He was determined to find us exactly the house we needed. Suddenly the fantasy began to take on ominous overtones of reality. Were we really going to go house hunting? It seemed we were.

Bring on the villages

Four long, hot days of trudging round St. Rémy ensued, in the course of which our friendship with Jean-Jacques was cemented over many a cold beer, but no likely property emerged. St. Rémy, it seemed, was out of the question. Everything we liked, we couldn't afford. Everything we could afford needed prohibitive work done on it.

Patrick was at that time in the throes of redecorating, and virtually rebuilding, his company's offices in London. Every evening I would come home to tales of woe: the carpenter had disappeared, the plumber had knocked the wrong hole in the wrong wall, the bosses were getting restless. 'It's bad enough when I am just down the road,' he told me. How on earth can we supervise building works on a French house from 800 miles away?

Given what we later learned of French builders, this was eminently sensible. A house which needed a lot doing to it was out of the question.

Would we, said Jean-Jacques, consider the villages?

Now this was the time to cry '*Finie la comédie.*' The moment, if ever, to back out gracefully, leaving our fantasy intact. After all, we had never really meant to buy a house, had we?

Fine, we said. Bring on the villages, we said.

Two more hot and thirsty days later, we had at least firmed up our ideas of what the ideal property would have to offer. 'It must,' I told Jean-Jacques, 'have a garage, a terrace and a *boulangerie*.' Jean-Jacques blinked a bit: he hadn't quite got to grips with the English sense of humour. But he soon cottoned on to the fact that what we needed was shops within walking distance. No rural idylls in the middle of nowhere for us. We are city mice.

House after house was seen and rejected. Nothing came quite up to expectation, and the end of our holiday was drawing closer. Then one evening Jean-Jacques said, 'I have two more houses I think you might like. We can go and see them tomorrow.'

We managed to wheedle the addresses out of him. This was a great concession, because estate agents live in mortal fear that the potential buyer will do a private deal with the potential seller and cut the agency out.

We promised that we would do no more than suss out the villages and take a look at the houses from the outside, and we kept our word. Well almost: we sussed out *two* villages and looked at *one* house from the outside. The other house we completely failed to find. Considering that the village was tiny and the address was in the Rue de l'Eglise, this might seem unlikely. But despite our very best endeavours, and despite my cries of 'Look for the church!' we never did find the house that evening.

The next morning we drove back to that village, in Jean-Jacques's little Peugeot. All became clear: we had been looking on the wrong side of the road. Morbignan la Crèbe is sharply divided between the old and the new, and the road runs between.

Jean-Jacques duly turned right where we had turned left, drove up a narrow street between ancient houses, turned the corner (by - yes! - the church) and stopped. We got out of the car. On the corner of the church square and a road so narrow you could have spanned it with outstretched arms, stood the ugliest house I had ever seen.

It was clearly old, very old. It was clearly cobbled together out of what had been two houses. It rose slab-fronted from the street, acres of decaying, yellowish *crépis* (plaster) bisected by sundry phone and electricity cables. A ridiculous stone staircase flanked by a stunted tree rose ungracefully to a pocket-handkerchief front terrace littered with debris and encrusted with cat droppings.

I stopped dead in my tracks. 'Ohmigawd' thought Himself to himself (as he told me later), 'we've just bought a house.'

Why? There were prettier houses. There were certainly prettier villages – Morbignan in those days was, to put it politely, a little run-down. What made me fall so immediately, so irrevocably in love with this house in this village?

Did I see possibilities in the tree? In years to come it would grow so high in its quest for light that it was to be seen on Google Earth. Was I enchanted by the steps, crumbling and lichen-dappled though they were? Did I foresee their future when, cleaned and decorated with pots of scarlet geraniums, they would prompt visitors to exclaim 'What a lovely house!' before even setting foot over the threshold?

Who can tell? All I can say is, the heart wants what the heart wants.

And so, for all those not exactly convincing reasons, Himself was quite right when he concluded 'We've just bought a house.'

Of course, it took a bit longer than that. We did take the precaution of actually viewing the house I had so precipitately fallen in love with. The house, I was convinced, that had opened one eye when I walked in and remarked 'Well, you took your time getting here.'

And we did play the property buying game, disdaining the derisory amount the seller was asking, and then chewing our fingernails till he came up with a counter-offer. We knew, Jean-Jacques knew - and for all I can say the house knew - that we would have bought it at twice the price. But effectively, yes, we bought that house at first sight.

So, having signed our *compromis de vente* (the document which expresses our intention to buy), and promised to have the money ready by October, we reluctantly got on the road and made our way back to England. We hardly dared look at each other. Had we really done it? And how on earth were we going to afford it?

By the time we got back to the UK we had come to terms with the idea. Indeed, we were positively blasé about the whole thing. And when friends asked us if we had had a good holiday, and what had we done while away, we soon learned to reply nonchalantly 'Oh, you know, the usual: went to the beach. Had some good meals. Did a spot of sight-seeing. Bought a house.'

Like you do.

Ipswich tables bear no labels

'It's very... big, isn't it, the house?' Patrick peered at me over the top of the list, pages of which had already spilled off his knees and on to the floor. We were back in London on a typical English late-summer day; the rain hurled itself with vindictive spite against the rattling window panes. The sights, the smells, the scorching heat of the Languedoc were a fond but distant memory.

'Well, let's see,' I said, delighted to do the math again. 'There's the kitchen and living room, the main guest room, the second guest room and our bedroom. No, it's not really that big. It's just rather a sprawling house.'

'You're forgetting the Minstrel's Gallery,' he corrected me, 'not to mention the Spider Room, and then there's that place across the terrace.'

Ah, the Minstrel's Gallery, how could I forget that? It was one of the many, many things that made us fall so in love with the house in the first place. Now let's be clear about this: a minstrel's gallery it wasn't. It didn't overlook the *salon,* in fact it didn't overlook anything. But as you mounted the creaking wooden stairway you found to your left a pine-floored space, a tiny window in a deep embrasure, a door firmly shut on the horror beyond. Given to the fanciful naming of things, Himself and I immediately christened this the Minstrel's Gallery, our imaginations furnishing it with cosy chintz sofas, book shelves and reading lamps.

The 'horror beyond' was, of course, the Spider Room. It had no proper floor. It had no proper ceiling. It had no window, and monsters lurked in its dim corners. Little did we know how it would be transformed in the years to come – but that's a story for later.

Then there was the terrace. We had specified to Jean-Jacques, the friendly estate agent, that the house we bought must have a terrace. Not an easy task, in a tiny village whose houses crowd and jumble together in improbable conjunctions. Morbignan La Crèbe used to be a farming village, and our house, like so many others, followed the traditional pattern: the *cave* (or cellar) was actually the ground floor, and housed the animals. The first floor was the living area – hence the steps up to the front door – and the floor above was for storing animal feed. Luckily for us, the previous owners had done much of the conversion, putting in a staircase where once only a ladder existed, and converting the top floor to create two interconnecting bedrooms, the minstrel's gallery and, of course, the spider room. I think they ran out of enthusiasm at that point.

Napoleonic law is stringent about the division of property among heirs, which meant that many houses were split in strange ways, and had odd bits tacked on to them. All of which is to say that houses with terraces were rare in Morbignan.

When we first saw our house we very nearly didn't buy it after all. A terrace was a *sine qua non* of purchase. We had no garden or terrace in London. On the rare fine days we could only gaze longingly at that little patch of blue that flat-dwellers call the sky (thank you, Oscar). Of course, it went without saying that the terrace should have a reasonable degree of privacy.

15

So when Jean-Jacques proudly led us through the red-flagged *cuisine*, through the smoke-scented *salon*, and stood us in front of the window to admire *la terrasse*, our first reaction was one of dismay. 'But it's overlooked,' I cried, eyeing the building that faced us across no more than five metres of lichen-encrusted concrete. And then, in even more horror, 'No – it's communal!' And indeed there was a doorway opposite. An arched, stone-set door of no very great height.

'No,' said Jean-Jacques, 'it's yours.'

'What do you mean, ours?' I gibbered. Jean-Jacques explained that part of the house opposite did indeed, by some quirk of Napoleonic law, belong to this house. The two upper floors, from terrace level upwards, were included in the sale as part of 'our' house. The *cave* belonged to – and adjoined - the house around the corner. We later deduced that the space between the two properties had once been the street.

Beside me, Himself was fizzing and popping and demanding to know what was what. In those days he spoke no French and, thanks to the local accent, understood even less. Obviously as smitten with the house as I was, though not admitting it, he was equally determined not to buy a house with a shared terrace.

'Jean-Jacques says it's ours,' I explained with some bewilderment. No fool Jean-Jacques. He knew that with that first heart-stopping glance from street level we had come, seen and been conquered. Of course the house was ours. It was all over bar the *compromis de vente*.

This unexpected property bonus, which was to cause us so much grief in the future, naturally clinched the *affaire*. Two whole extra rooms! No matter that they were disused, grimy and scorpion-infested. No matter that from the lower window hung only mouldering shutters with no glass behind them. No matter that the upper window peered sightlessly at us through a rough-hewn hole in the wall. No matter that the *cave* belonged to someone else – to the very Notaire, in fact, before whom we would soon be signing the necessary papers. We could live with all that, couldn't we?

To return to rain-swept London: airily I dismissed the Minstrel's Gallery, the Spider room (shudder!) and the outhouses. 'We'll deal with those in good time,' I promised brightly. 'Let's just get the basics in place.'

And so began the hunt, the squeezing of pennies, the buttering-up of family. The local second-hand furniture shops were raided on a daily basis. Friends had amazing attics which produced lamps and wall cupboards and even bits of carpeting at an astonishing rate. Other, skilful friends sewed curtains and cushion covers. Parents reluctantly parted with cherished tables and arm chairs; jumble sales yielded space heaters and wind chimes, glass jugs and fireplace companion sets. In mounting excitement we bought presents for the house: lamp shades, waste bins, a glass-fronted pine cabinet (I have it still), pictures and soap dishes and a whole new set of bright red saucepans.

And then there was Ipswich. Ipswich, and East Anglia in general, is the car boot sale capital. Close friends of ours lived in that exciting location and, generous and sympathetic allies that they were, they invited us to stay with them on a regular basis. It was a treasure trove, and cheap beyond the dreams of avarice. Week by week our store of booty accumulated; our

London dining room became a furniture repository as we steadfastly refused to confront the problem of how we were going to get it all across the channel.

The date of our return to France was coming ever closer. We'd decided to go back to Morbignan in October and sign the paperwork ourselves, rather than allow Jean-Jacques to act as proxy, which had been the original plan. What had we been thinking? We were never going to pass up the excitement of sitting in the *Notaire's cabinet* and putting pen to paper on the deeds. Our store of furnishings, which we were planning to take with us, was almost complete. All that was missing was a kitchen table.

'Should we give James and Rosemary a call?' I said tentatively. We were rather afraid we had worn our welcome thin in Ipswich. And then the phone rang. 'Rosemary here,' came the cheerful, familiar bellow. 'Would you like to come up next weekend?'

So it was that once again we set off on the car boot trail, this time with a very precise brief: to find a kitchen table that matched my exact specifications. We ransacked two sales without success, but on the third we struck gold. Half hidden under a pile of boxed jigsaw puzzles (you just knew that several pieces were missing) it sat forlorn and dusty: wooden, solid, rustic and aged.

The stall owner was reluctant at first to drag it out, but seeing the gleam of acquisition in our eyes he relented. The table was everything I could have wished. Folded up, it didn't take up too much space, but two leaves extended to make reasonably comfortable seating for six. The wooden crossbar joining the legs was scuffed and gouged - I pictured generations of farmers coming in from the fields for their midday meal and resting their booted feet on the bar. It was priced at a princely £20, and we were so enthralled with our find that we didn't even haggle.

Back in London, and with departure only a few days away, I took another woman's husband to lunch. Arthur, a director with the television company I then worked for, was the husband of my Manchester-based friend and colleague. His job took him to London regularly and I was sometimes given the great treat of lunching with him. His kindness was legendary, his sense of humour off the scale. On this occasion I was chattering on interminably about the house and our purchases, and, very patiently, he listened with every semblance of fascination.

Suddenly, though, his face fell. 'Where did you say you bought that table,' he asked sternly. And, when I told him, his expression darkened. 'Was that wise,' he asked in Eeyore tones. 'Don't you know about Ipswich tables?'

As I shook my head, he explained: 'Ipswich tables bear no labels.' And, completely straight-faced, he launched into a five-minute impromptu speech about the perils of buying tables in Ipswich. I giggled, then I howled. The waiter rushed over in consternation: why was the lady at table six crying?

And forevermore, whenever the subject of tables, and in particular kitchen tables, was raised, Himself and I would catch each other's eye and mouth 'Ipswich tables.'

The long road south

On Friday October 23rd 1987, a little over four years after that first holiday in St Rémy des Cévennes, Patrick and I closed the door on our London flat and embarked on an adventure that was to last for 27 years. At the end of it, our lives would be transformed beyond all recognition. Of course, we knew none of that at the time. All we knew was that we were setting out, with enormous excitement, to complete the formalities and furnish and settle in to our new holiday home in the Pays d'Oc.

Weeks of frantic activity had preceded this moment. First came the agonising: how on earth were we going to transport what had become a medium-sized furniture repository to the south of France without the aid of a pantechnicon? Easy, said Himself, hire a long-wheelbase Ford Transit. It was the first time these words had entered my ken, but it was not to be the last. Himself adores large vehicles, be they Land Rovers or Transit vans, and will seize on any excuse to jump behind the wheel of one. And, just to be on the safe side, we had also borrowed a trailer.

Then a more savvy friend put me wise to *les permis*. Innocents that we were, we thought that transporting half a ton of assorted tables, chairs, lampshades and bath mats into France – a newly-acquired partner in the great adventure of the EEC – would be a breeze. What were we thinking? If there is one thing that makes a French official's eyes light up with glee it is an unauthorised undertaking. Paperwork must be completed in triplicate. *Tampons* (rubber stamps) must be applied with vigour. And a spot of grovelling does not go amiss.

First I had to consult the French consulate in London. Yes, of course, they said, you may take your furniture to France, but there is paperwork... Two days later, after much head-scratching, the document was complete and had to be sanctioned – by the authorities in France. And quick, sharp, too, as the date of our departure was fast approaching and no way would we be allowed into the country without the necessary rubber stamps. I bundled the package into a fat brown envelope (taking care to copy the lot, illicitly, on the office photocopier) and found a courier firm. Oh, yes, they said, they'd pick it up at midday from my office, take it to France, get the required signatures and it would be back with me within 48 hours.

It didn't quite go that way. In my naiveté I thought when the nice lady on despatch said 'We'll send a courier to pick it up at 12 o'clock' that she actually meant that very day. So I duly left my precious parcel with the friendly commissionaire at the front desk, explaining that it would be collected at noon. At three o'clock Jeff put his head round my door. 'It's still at the front desk,' he said apologetically. 'Perhaps you should give them a ring?' Strangely, when I rang the couriers, there was no reply.

But yes, the parcel was indeed collected at noon – 24 hours later. 'I've discovered what DHL means,' I reported bitterly to Himself. 'Don't Hurry, Lads.'

Still, the papers eventually winged themselves back to us, all nicely signed and stamped, and we were all set to go. Apart from one tiny thing.

'You'll need an inventory,' counselled the same savvy friend, who had already been through the whole bureaucratic process. 'And make sure it's detailed, if you want to get through customs without too much delay.'

And that's when I decided to out-French the French. Taking a deep breath and a large notebook I plunged into the depths of what had been our dining room. Two hours later I emerged, bleary-eyed but satisfied with my labours. 'Two arm chairs, leather,' I had written. 'One sofa, matching arm chairs; three side tables; two lamps with brown ceramic bases; two lamps with orange ceramic bases, five drinking glasses, green, small; six drinking glasses, green, large; six knives with red handles; six forks with red handles; six dessert spoons with red handles; five tea spoons with red handles…' and so it went on, for page after page. Not a jot or a tittle, had we possessed such a thing, would have been omitted. Once more the trusty office photocopier was called on, and the whole list was reproduced in triplicate.

There would come a time when I was grateful for such punctiliousness.

Suddenly D (for departure) Day was only 72 hours away. Facing the prospect of loading up several tons of assorted furniture we quailed. Then, 'Let's have a breakfast party,' said Patrick happily one morning over toast and wrangling. I looked at him as if he'd lost his senses. Had the whole business unhinged him, I wondered. Then the beauty of the plan began to take hold. For the price of a few croissants, a litre or two of orange juice and lots and lots of strong coffee, we could assemble our more gullible friends – especially those with strong arms and backs, and enlist their help.

It went without a hitch. Thursday October 22nd dawned cold and cloudy, but dry. By eight o'clock our friends Lin and Chang had arrived, sleeves rolled up and ready for business. Soon others, including Himself's hapless brother who had been corralled into helping at the last minute, were busy heaving and complaining and shouting and quarrelling and scoffing croissants at an alarming rate (I had to run up the road twice for more) - but above all loading our possessions for their journey to the sun. 'It'll never all go in there' I wailed, but I was wrong. The capacity of a Transit with Luton (I learned that day that a Luton is the bit over the cab, useful for storing odd-shaped bits and pieces) rivals that of a Tardis. With the addition of an Ifor Williams trailer (kindly lent by Himself's brother) every last knife, fork and spoon was eventually stowed.

By one o'clock it was done. We took everyone out for a celebratory Indian lunch and sent them on their way. The afternoon, we had planned, was for resting and recuperating before we set off the next morning. Instead, of course, we fidgeted, squabbled, had doubts, resolved doubts, consulted lists a dozen times, checked a dozen times that, yes, we had remembered the space heater and the new shower curtains, until finally we crawled into bed to fret the rest of the night away.

Friday was bright and sunny. A good omen, I thought, but Himself looked less than pleased. I soon found out why: the road from London to Dover heads south-east, and at that time of day, at that time of year, that meant driving directly into the sun. The entire journey we spent squinting and peering at the road ahead trying desperately to avoid running into anything. It considerably slowed what was already going to be a long, slow journey.

We eventually reached Dover without mishap and, driving down that long curving road that leads to the harbour, we were in time to see the graceful white shape of a ferry negotiating the harbour gates on its way to France. Unfortunately, it was *our* ferry.

An hour and a half later, after a kindly despatcher had squeezed us on to the next available boat – it was practically empty – we were finally under way.

At Calais we lumbered off the ferry and, ignoring a small official with a large hat who kept bellowing '*Fret! Fret!*' at us, we made our determined way to the domestic immigration channel. The small official pursued us, and when he paused for breath I explained politely that, no, we weren't freight: we were an inoffensive English couple taking some household goods to a *maison secondaire*. We had all the paperwork, I added helpfully. For a second this gave the small official pause, then he brightened. '*Douanes, Douanes*' he said, gesturing towards a dilapidated hut off to one side of the docks. Dutifully, we made our way to the *Douanes*, the customs shed.

The customs officer peered disdainfully through his little window at the dusty Ford Transit sagging on its springs, at the laden trailer with here a chair leg, there a lamp shade poking out from beneath its insecurely tied tarp. Ignoring the fact that I had spoken to him in French, 'Do you heff an eeenventory?' he sneered.

Did I have an inventory? Mentally blessing my savvy friend and the office photocopier, I produced the paperwork. It ran to 27 pages; it was written in English with a French translation for each item. It landed on the ledge with a satisfying thump.

'*Mon dieu!*' The customs officer smoothed his moustache with an agitated finger, '*Passez, passez!*'

We waited until we were a kilometre or two beyond the docks before we allowed ourselves the explosion of laughter we felt was our due.

24

The ensuing two and a half days set the pattern for so many journeys over the next 25 years that it has blurred from memory. Yes, it was long, and tedious, and no-one had told us that while an elderly Transit, which was all we could afford to hire, had a theoretical top speed of 55 mph, by the time it was loaded with assorted household goods we would be lucky to see 45 downhill with a following wind.

Still, we were buoyed up with excitement and the steadily improving weather, and by the time we were having lunch at the Arche motorway services near Montpellier – on the roof terrace! In shirtsleeves! In October! – we were ecstatic.

Then we arrived.

There is a cartoon which has always made me laugh: two Daleks standing at the foot of a staircase. One of them is saying: 'Well, that buggers up our plan to conquer the universe.' On that day in October 1987 we knew just how it felt. What hadn't occurred to us, while we were shouting encouragement and doling out croissants two and a half days earlier, was that in France there would be no willing, laughing band of friends to do the work for us. It was just us, and a staircase. Yes, that same ramshackle set of stone steps which had so enchanted me the day we first saw the house. It was still there – and it stood between our van-load of furniture and our new home.

One or two locals began to drift up to see what was afoot. Aha, I thought, now we'll get some help. I was wrong. They were happy to exchange smiles. Some even ventured a '*Bonjour, vous vous installez*?' ('Hello. You are moving in?' The French have a genius for stating the obvious). But no offer of assistance was forthcoming. We were the day's entertainment: in a tiny rural village in October you take what you can get.

Soon we had attracted a small crowd. Patrick, rather bitterly, suggested we hand out inventories, in case there was some trifling item of our personal belongings the spectators had missed. Meanwhile, metaphorically rolling up our shirt sleeves, we got on with the heavy lifting.

Somehow, some two or three hours later, everything was either stowed in the ground-floor garage or stacked on the red stone flags of our new kitchen. Everything, that is, except the sideboard. I'd fallen in love with it in an antique-cum-junk shop in West Hampstead. Old, battered, charming – and enormous.

And now here it was at the foot of our steps, far too heavy for just the two of us to lift. Himself is the practical one. He hummed. He hawed. He walked round

26

the offending article scratching his head and looking wise. Then, 'Why don't we roll it up, end over end?' I piped up.

I'll never forget the look on his face. The words 'don't worry your pretty little head about it: this is man's work' were simply *bursting* to be spoken. Then he paused. His eyes widened with incredulity. 'That's not such a bad idea' he conceded. Wrapped in a blanket, our precious sideboard was solemnly rolled, end over end, up the stone staircase, over the rather high sill, and into the kitchen. There was a collected sigh from the onlookers – I half expected applause.

It was my moment of glory, and I've never let Himself forget it.

TWO:

Maison

Secondaire

We were going to be the ideal neighbours. We would be pleasant and welcoming when acquaintances dropped in just as we were getting supper ready. We would sweep our front steps regularly. We would shop in the village épicerie and employ local tradesmen.

We would be nothing like 'les marginaux' - those other, awful English grape-pickers who had rampaged drunkenly through the streets half a decade ago.

We were going to be 'des gens correctes'.

Lights! Action! Neighbours!

'Wuff!' with a final heave Himself slid the sideboard into place and stood back to admire his labours. The kitchen was transformed. The house was transformed. And, dare I say it, Patrick was transformed. Never before (or since) had I witnessed such a flurry of activity as that of the past three days. Back at home, if I mentioned that perhaps an extra set of hooks on the kitchen wall might make life easier, I could be sure they would be put up. Eventually. Probably. It might be six months later, after I had made the request and forgotten all about it, that suddenly Himself would resurrect his enthusiasm for DIY and make with the screwdriver.

Morbignan, it seemed, had wrought miracles. A new wall cupboard here? Done. A shelf over the sink? No problem. Coat hooks behind the door? Yep, there they are. In three days our enchanting - but cold, dusty and inconvenient – little house had become something we were beginning to think of as home.

A word about the French and convenience. They don't do it. Or, at least, not to British expectations. I still remember with a kind of horrified affection the small Paris hotel where the room door led straight into the loo, which you had to cross to get to the bedroom. Here in Morbignan, at least it was only the guest room you had to traverse to get to the master bedroom.

Then there was the matter of the kitchen light. Our front door opened into the kitchen, which in those early days was lit only by a dim bulb hanging from the centre of the ceiling. Not a problem, one might have thought: the addition of a 100-watt bulb would improve things enormously. The real snag was the light switch. Inside the front door? Not a bit of it. The light switch for the kitchen was across the room, beside the door leading into the salon.

Now the house was several hundred years old, and it was a safe bet that for at least fifty years it had had electricity. So for half a century the house's owners had trudged and stumbled their way from the front door, across the kitchen – never light at the best of times but pitch-black in winter – to switch on the light.

Even Himself could see there was something wrong. Scribbling hieroglyphs on the back of envelopes (he swore they were wiring diagrams) and muttering something which sounded alarmingly like bi-polar, he set to work. Three hours later our brand-new switch was *in situ*, and we could actually turn on the kitchen light both from the salon and from the front door. This I learned, incidentally, was the meaning of bi-polar: nothing at all to do with mental disturbance, which was a relief.

Some days later, when we proudly invited the house's former owners in for coffee, we showed them the improvement. Monsieur blinked a bit. '*Ah, oui…très bien.*' And yet, somehow, I don't think he was impressed.

Of course the lighting improved in very short order. Spotlights over the sink and cooker, a rustic lamp to add *ambience* to our dinner table, all these innovations were regarded with much dubiosity by our local friends. Still, they consoled themselves, '*Ce sont des anglais.*' You had to make allowances for such eccentrics.

Ce sont des anglais. Oh, there was a wealth of meaning in those words. It might be condemnation: what can you expect from such barbarians? *Perfide Albion* coming to *our* village and buying *our* houses (at greatly inflated prices) and spending their filthy money in *our* shops. Or it might be a rueful tolerance: well, they're foreign, poor things, they don't know how it's done. The *anglais* tag we would never lose. The trick, I learned, was to be regarded as *des gens correctes*.

On the whole, the English were historically not well looked upon in Morbignan. For years some of the more disreputable of our countrymen had descended on the village in September to work on the *vendange*, the grape harvest. Lodged, for the most part, in barns and outhouses and paid a pittance, they had nothing to thank their French hosts for, so it was understandable if not forgivable that they took their pleasures where they could. Wine was the cheapest drink available, and this they consumed with gusto. Local girls were fair game and an evening's entertainment at the café usually included a fight, with or without knives.

By the time we arrived in the village all this had largely gone by the board. The tall, narrow, alarmingly tottering *vendange* machines had superseded the merry bands of grape pickers, and peace was restored to Morbignan's September days. But, as I mentioned, there was a lingering mistrust of anyone from across the Channel.

Naturally, the locals had taken a keen interest in our *installation*. The mayor stopped by to introduce himself. The plumber called to see if we needed assistance – we did. Every time we ventured out on to our minuscule front terrace, there on the street below were three or four neighbours, who had just happened to have paused for a moment to exchange *bonjours*, enormously surprised to see us and yes, well, we might just be able to spare a moment to take coffee with you. And have a good nosy, I

34

thought, as I filled yet another cafetière, which surprised them no end: cafetières in rural France, it seems, are confined to posh cafés. 'At home we boil the grounds in a saucepan on the kitchen stove, but, hey, *ce sont des anglais.*'

It was all part of a carefully planned campaign. We were going to be the ideal neighbours. We would be pleasant and welcoming when acquaintances dropped in just as we were getting supper ready. We would sweep our front steps regularly. We would shop in the village *épicerie* and employ local tradesmen. Patrick would sit – but strictly only by invitation – on the bench in the square with the Good Ol' Boys of the village. We would be nothing like *les marginaux* - those other, awful English who had rampaged drunkenly through the streets half a decade ago.

We were going to be *des gens correctes.*

Seating solutions

The trouble with being *des gens correctes* is that it's hard work. Day four of our installation saw us once again cleaning and polishing, rearranging furniture, arguing about what went where (why couldn't Himself see that the only place for the wine glasses was in the glass-fronted cabinet over the fridge?) and going to the phone every three minutes to see if, at last, we were connected. We needed some R&R.

We also needed something else.

We'd depleted Ipswich. We'd crammed our dining room to bursting point. We had painstakingly made lists and inventories. We thought we had it covered.

But there's always that thing, isn't there? That glaringly obvious thing that you can't, you surely can't have overlooked. In our case it was dining chairs. Oh, we had something to sit on. There was the bentwood chair, painted a startling orange, that I had bought for my first-ever student flat at a cost of six shillings. There was the old wooden armchair we found in the 'studio' (as we grandly named it) across the terrace, rickety but serviceable. And we had a kitchen stool, tall and spindly, which left your legs dangling if you were anything under six feet tall.

Bottoms, then, were catered for, up to a point. But we wanted more for our new home – something gracious and welcoming, rustic and charming. Something to grace a candle-lit dinner party, with the wine and conversation sparkling round the table.

The French have a lovely phrase that you'll hear trumpeted over the town-hall loud speakers every market day: *une visite s'impose.* What it means is that you must, you really must visit this stall, this purveyor of *coquillages* or other attraction. In our case, a visit to the local *brocante* really did impose itself.

St Rémy des Cévennes is blessed with many antique shops; in fact, there is a whole street of them. To stroll down it is to see your every need, your every wish, your every fantasy fulfilled. Do you need a perambulator, an occasional table, a slightly lopsided standard lamp? Perhaps your fancy turns to a twelve-foot high wrought-iron giraffe or a sewing box with "*Maman*" in pokerwork on the lid. Chairs there are a-plenty: upright or upholstered, dining or kitchen, tiny children's chairs and stately carvers, sagging canvas recliners and overstuffed loungers.

Of course, the French have a rather relaxed attitude to the word *brocante*: it covers a multitude of sins, from dignified, beeswax-scented emporia to the grottiest of second-hand furniture shops. In those early days we were still innocent of the out-of-town possibilities of *le troc* and *la trocante* – something between a furniture store and a pawnshop – and perhaps that was just as well. As it was, we had an embarrassment of riches right there in St Rémy.

We walked up the street, we walked down it, and then we walked back up again, bewildered by choice. Eventually we picked on one shop which looked approachable: not so opulent as to be beyond our price range, not so seedy that we feared fleas. Venturing inside we found the place deserted. It was quite a relief: no danger of being pounced on before we were ready.

After five minutes I found what I thought we were looking for: a wooden dining chair with a curlicued back and spindly legs. Its cane seat gave it just the right cottagey look to complement our kitchen. And standing next to this treasure were two more. They had cane seats and curlicued backs and spindly legs, right enough, but the curlicues were different and the legs spindled the other way round – not just from the first chair, but from each other as well. Aha, we thought, such charming eccentricity is bound to be a talking point.

Next came the problem of winkling Monsieur out of his lair. From a cubbyhole at the back of the shop we could hear the roars and jeers of a television – evidently some kind of football match was in progress. We loitered politely for a while, as English people do, and then I decided enough was enough. 'Monsieur?' I queried politely. No response. I repeated the question *crescendo*, until eventually on a lung-splitting bellow of 'MONSIEUR' the proprietor emerged, can of Kronenbourg in one hand, the remains of a sandwich in the other. He looked surprised to see us.

We explained that we wanted to buy some chairs. He looked even more surprised. Perhaps we were the only customers to cross his threshold that day… or that week? We liked the chairs, I told him, but we needed six. Did he have any more in the same style? He grinned, and beckoned, 'Follow me'.

Pushing aside a lamp standard, a dusty *clic-clac* (sofa bed) and a small table tottering with books, he opened a door and proudly stood back to let us admire. It was a cavernous room, thick with cobwebs and redolent of dust, piled high with furniture of every description. How on earth you'd find anything in this space was beyond us, but Monsieur knew his stock.

He led us on a circuitous path through the dimness – how the French adore their 40-watt light bulbs – to a corner where stood at least a couple of dozen chairs similar to those we had seen in the shop. No two were alike, or so we hoped: we had set our hearts on eccentricity. Could we, we asked, see them in daylight? *'Bien sûr'* was the reply. He picked up two of the chairs and set off back the way we had come. Emboldened, Himself and I collected a further two apiece and followed him.

Of the nine chairs we had assembled four were identical, two more were identical to each other but not to the first four, and three looked nothing like the others. Gingerly we tested them: all seemed sound enough and promised to bear Himself's not inconsiderable weight quite safely.

Now there was just the question of design. We separated out five with cane seats, different curlicued backs and different spindly legs. Could we, we asked Monsieur apologetically, see some more? He nodded understandingly, but warned that he'd bought them in a job lot from a hotel: it might be difficult to find six chairs all the same.

Actually, we want eight, I told him, and we want them all different. He looked perplexed for a moment, then he grinned. *'Ah oui,'* said his expression, *'Ce sont des Anglais.'*

Back we plunged into the dusty depths and six more chairs emerged. A lot of head scratching, muttering and careful comparison ensued, at the end of which we had seven individual chairs and one match. I hardly dared ask, but… *'Pas de problème,'* cried Monsieur with the bit between his teeth. A final six were brought out and at last, wonder of wonders, the disparate collection was complete.

After many grins and handshakes what seemed like an embarrassingly small amount of money was exchanged and we had our dining set. Remained the problem of getting it home. 'What a good job we have a Transit,' said Himself meaningfully. He never missed an opportunity to point out what a splendid idea it would be for us to own a van, or at the very least an exceedingly large Land Rover.

'Yes, dear,' I said.

L'Hipocrape est mort

'They must be rich,' said the uninitiated, 'they have two houses.' 'Ah no,' said the savvy, 'they have two houses: they must be exceedingly poor.'

The savvy had the right of it. Two houses to furnish, two sets of local taxes, two lots of heating bills to face, not to mention the cost of a 1,500-mile round trip to France two or three times a year – even in the affluent eighties that was a considerable burden to bear.

Then there are the thousand and one things you suddenly realise you need, once you have moved in; from a lemon squeezer to a duvet set, from a doormat to a bathroom cabinet.

And so, like Autolycus in "The Winter's Tale", we became snappers-up of unconsidered trifles. We raided car boot sales in England and *vide-greniers* in France, we loitered hopefully when friends were decluttering, we developed a sharp eye for the main chance.

Take, for example, the day when, back in London once more, I was standing at the bus stop, on my way to town for a lunch meeting. I was hoping to snaffle the job of publicising a new television series that my client, an independent producer, had just pitched successfully to Channel 4. Dressed to impress in heels and a sharp suit, recently acquired on a trip to the US, I had left my car boot head at home along with my less-than-elegant working attire: leggings and a sloppy sweater.

Right next to the bus stop stood a junk shop. You couldn't call it anything else: the windows were obscured with grime and cobwebs, the door sagged off its hinges and an aroma of decay wafted into the street. But – and my eyes lit up like a beacon – there in the window stood a convector heater. Surely a very *cheap* convector heater.

Our lovely French home devoured heaters. In the summer, when the temperature soared into the 30s, the thick stone walls and tiled floors gave sweet relief from the heat. But we were in love – we wanted to be there all the year round. And while this wasn't possible, we did manage to squeeze in several trips a year, and not all of them in summer. In the autumn and winter Morbignan could be quite cold – and then stone walls and tiled floors were not so welcoming. The more heaters we bought, the more we seemed to need.

We'd exhausted all our friends' generosity, we'd cleaned out the local jumble sales of every heater they could provide. And now here was another one, beckoning me through generations of dust. It was no good: I had to enquire.

Foregoing the approaching bus, risking being late for my meeting, I went into the shop. How much, I asked, was the heater displayed in the window? 'Oh, it doesn't work,' came the reply. 'We can't sell it.'

Channelling my very best Autolycus I snapped back 'Well, if it doesn't work, then I can have it for free, can't I?' I reckoned, rightly as it turned out, that Patrick could repair in no time flat. As it turned out, the plug merely needed a new fuse.

The shopkeeper was so stunned that he agreed to let me have the heater for no money; and so it was that the smart lunchers of London were treated to the spectacle of a fashionably booted and suited young lady staggering into the trendy Tandoori Mahal in Soho clutching an ancient, filthy and decrepit convector heater.

My client gave me the job on the spot.

But all this pales into insignificance compared to the story of l'Hipocrape.

We were on one of our many holidays in the Languedoc, and my London friend Lin had come over on a visit. Lin is the acquisition queen; she puts me in the shade. She finds treasure where the rest of us see rubbish. I still have the little round table she found left out with the dustbins. I still remember the day she swept up a potted plant clearly "abandoned" on the pavement, only to be pursued hotly by the restaurant owner, whose plant it was.

We had gone into St Rémy one evening and were strolling back from *apéros* at our favourite café, "*l'Ane des Cévennes*", on a leisurely quest for dinner. Himself and our neighbour Alice were walking a few steps ahead, when suddenly Lin stopped dead in her tracks. Her eyes lit up. 'An ironing board!' she trumpeted. 'Didn't you say you needed an ironing board?'

Well no, actually, I hadn't, and I didn't. Ironing was something other people did, a pure waste of time in my book. But as I aspired to be seen as a *bonne ménagère* – the female of the species *gens correctes* – I supposed I ought at least to possess an ironing board. And here was one such, lying abandoned by the side of the road.

Himself had wandered back to see what the hold-up was, and I explained that we had found an ironing board – *just* the thing I needed. Patrick took a look. He poked, he prodded, he delivered his verdict: 'It's a heap of crap.'

I was having none of it. 'No, it's perfectly good,' I insisted. 'It just needs a new cover. Give me the keys, I'm going to take it to the car, then I'll join you at the restaurant.'

Now, as every woman will immediately recognise, this was wife-speak. Himself is nothing if not a gentleman, and my proposing to carry a whole ironing board all by myself was unthinkable. So when I said 'I will take it to the car' I was actually saying 'You will take it to the car for me, but of course I am going to let you think you volunteered.'

Patrick picked up the board and trotted off down the street with an expression which clearly said, 'Don't blame me: this wasn't my idea.' To add insult to injury, the car was parked at the far end of town, and Himself had to run the gamut of cheers and jeers from the terraces of the many cafes he passed. He was not best pleased.

With the offending article finally stowed in the boot of the car we resumed our dinner plans. 'What is ironing board in French?' asked Lin, who regards me as the fount of knowledge of all things French. I hesitated. There is a perfectly good French word for ironing board: it's *une planche à repasser*. But, with Himself's comment in mind, I had a better idea. 'Oh, it's *un hipocrape*,' I said.

We took the ironing board home and I installed it proudly in the cupboard under the stairs. I didn't expect to see it again – it was enough that I owned it. But, as chance would have it, three days later the village was celebrating *Le Quatorze* – Bastille Day – with a communal feast and dancing in the square. It's a grand occasion, and everybody wears their finest clothes, never mind that they inevitably get snagged on splintery benches and splashed with *mariniere* sauce.

Lin and I duly trotted out our gay apparel and looked at it in some dismay. My strappy sundress had dropped to the bottom of the wardrobe and curled itself into a ball – it was creased beyond belief. Lin had left her ruffled blouse in her suitcase – it looked as if a cat had

44

slept on it. Even by the *laissez-faire* standards of Morbignan, they clearly would not do. It was time to wake l'Hipocrape from its slumber.

We duly took it out and set it up. I had taken the precaution of removing its decidedly tatty cover and buying it a new one in Intermarché, gaily patterned in blue and yellow to match the kitchen. 'You go first,' said Lin, and I'll go and have a shower.' Was this simple generosity, or did she suspect something?

I carefully smoothed the dress's skirt in place. I tested the iron to make sure it wasn't too hot. I firmly applied iron to skirt. There was a kind of hiss, a slithery, crackly sort of noise, and one leg of the ironing board gave way beneath me. It was riddled with woodworm.

Was Himself smug? Was Himself gleeful? Did he dance round the kitchen chanting; 'I *told* you it was a heap of crap'? Discretion forbids me to comment.

The next day, of course, was *férié* – this was the holiday of the 14th of July when nothing opens for at least a week. But as soon normal business resumed we took a trip to the *décharge* – the local tip.

In those days, before recycling, before eco-mania, you simply tossed your detritus into a pit, let the scavengers take what they would. Himself held the Hipocrape aloft. I got out my camera: before he hurled it into oblivion I would take a commemorative photo.

Much later, I pasted that picture into an album. The caption was simple and dignified: *l'Hipocrape est mort.*

Party politics

Our new dining chairs stood gleaming softly in the lamplight, their cane seats and gracious curves lending an air of elegance to the workaday kitchen. What we didn't notice was that they were lending something else: a gentle feathering of dust was accumulating on the floor beneath them, courtesy of the busy woodworm within.

All too soon would come the dash to Conforama, via the *décharge*, where we would pause for an instant in quiet contemplation at the grave of the Hipocrape. All too soon a set of solid, workmanlike chairs would grace our kitchen table.

But all that was to come. Now, in the first flush of new ownership, we wanted to celebrate our *brocante* treasure in its new setting.

'I know. Let's have a party,' I said.

Back in the heady eighties, when we wore designer suits and ate expense account lunches, Patrick and I were inveterate party givers. The cocktail party, the Breakfast Club, Divine Decadence, Lunatic Fringe, Pats 'n Plebs, Trivial Pursuit; our parties have become legendary. That is to say, every once in a while one of our friends might remark, 'Do you remember when…'

But we didn't do it for fame, nor fortune, we did it for fun. The planning, the guest lists, the drink, the food – it was engrossing, all-consuming. In the days when "Brideshead Revisited" was all the rage we spent an hour dyeing quails' eggs green (to match the green champagne). When Divine Decadence proved a step too far for some of our more timorous friends, they dropped out like flies, leaving only the stalwarts, two of whom came as a Borgia pope and a fallen nun. Right, we thought, these few, these happy few will be our inner party circle. We planned the Lunatic Fringe with them in mind. A select gathering for an evening of even more improbable romps. And one by one our timorous friends sidled up and muttered, from the side of their mouths, 'Can we come too, please?'

Parties in Morbignan la Crèbe, we were to learn, were different. Oh, no less riotous – wine was cheap, ex-pats rowdy and holidaying natives can let their hair down with the best of them – but different: more seasonal, confined to a smaller locale and hence more fraught with dangers. To begin with, they all fell within the purlieus of The Season. The Season proper starts with *Le Quatorze* - Bastille Day - the glorious Fourteenth of July when the French desert the industrial north and head for the lazy south. Every year some bright spark would trot out that old hoary chestnut: 'Will the last person leaving Paris please turn out the lights?'

Come the last weekend of August, come *La Rentrée*. Suddenly beach mats and portable fans in Intermarché are replaced by schoolbags and exercise books whose pages are divided into squares, not lines. The grapes hang heavy and luscious on the vines and the word *vendange* is beginning to be heard. It's even possible to park in the village again, as the summer visitors trickle homewards.

The Season is over, but, oh, the parties we have had in those six hedonistic weeks! The *apéros* – the little drinks parties, whether impromptu or planned. The barbecue inevitably interrupted, even in the best of summers, by the spectacular thunderstorm. The great big thrash we'd spent months planning and agonising over.

Why did we do it? What was it that drove us to pore despairingly over guest lists, trot out the mini vol-au-vents, dust the skirting boards and, worst of all, brave the politics?

The politics of parties, as any host or hostess will tell you, are enough to make brave men weep and strong women quail. Who is an item at the moment? Who is at daggers drawn? Who will be mortally offended if invited (or not invited) to the same party as whom?

There are ways and ways of dealing with it all. The simplest, of course, would be not to have a party at all. But we never learn. So, as a veteran of many a campaign, let me offer my take on how to survive The Season relatively unscathed. There are, as I see it, three ways of going about it: the Thrash, the Impromptu and the Select.

The Thrash is the easiest, and the hardest, solution. It's easy because you just invite everyone. Never mind that Jean-Luc hasn't spoken to Marie Claire since that business with the poodle. Never mind that Bernard's wife has been exchanging glances with Benito and Bernard is getting restless. Just invite 'em all and let them sort themselves out - or *se débrouiller* as the locals might say.

That way, there's no danger of a chance remark in the bar – 'We'll see you at *Untel*'s ("*Untel*" is the French equivalent of "so and so") on Sunday, won't we?' – leading to an 'oops!' situation. That way, the invitation issued in a wine-induced burst of bonhomie to someone you can't stand doesn't really matter. You can always lose them in the crowd. But of course there are drawbacks. The planning, the hard work, the stress, and always that special little incident that makes the whole thing memorable. Wincingly memorable. The night that two partygoers, deeply preoccupied with one another, fell headlong down the terrace steps. The morning we came down to find two guests – *sans* their respective partners - blissfully asleep entwined on the canapé.

At one Thrash Himself, who does not keep late hours, retired peacefully to bed at about one o'clock. At three I followed, leaving the remnants to look after themselves. We are hospitable and open-minded people, but there are limits to even our tolerance. At four a.m. our well-lubricated guests decided to serenade us from the terrace, which is directly beneath our bedroom window. After a few minutes of this Himself rose in wrath and, uttering a mild expletive or two, chucked them out. He's been known as Mr Grumpy ever since – affectionately, we think - but we survived the Party Politics trap.

The Impromptu is a good alternative. You've gathered in the bar for a couple of pre-prandials, and suddenly it seems a jolly good wheeze to invite everyone back to yours for a bite to eat. Somehow this never happens when the house is tidy and you have a larder full of stuff – you frantically rack your brains as to what you can do with some leftover potatoes, an old onion and a can of tuna fish – but that's all part of the fun.

In true loaves-and-fishes style, everyone contributes what they have and you all muck in together. Of course, it usually tends to be the same people every time, but then after all they are your closest friends, aren't they?

The Select is the most fun for all concerned, but fraught with peril. The idea of this is that you hold several small gatherings throughout the holiday period. The 'plus' side is obvious. They are more manageable. You get to talk to people rather than dashing wild-eyed through the crush trying to make sure everyone has a drink and someone to talk to. You choose among your friends a guest list which will provide everyone with someone new to meet as well as a few familiar faces. Like-minded people who don't know each other can be introduced. The odd maverick choice will spice things up nicely.

But oh, the danger, the danger! No matter how discreet you are, word will get out that you are having a 'do'. Friends who have been invited want to know why to this particular gathering. Friends who haven't been invited will want to know the same thing. The words 'A' List will be muttered darkly in corners. But on the whole, in spite of all the *angst*, I'd plump for the Select any day. It has one shining advantage over the others. By the time the Season is over nobody is speaking to you, and you'll never have to have another party.

Innocents that we were when we first moved in, all this was ahead of us. We knew nothing of the reefs and shoals of festive entertaining, that day when I stood in the kitchen in Morbignan and, fed up with trying to remove some sinister-looking stains from the red-tiled floor, suggested brightly: 'let's have a party.'

Did we know anyone? Of course not. Were we going to let that stop us? Of course not. There was the nice estate agent – and his brother-in-law, their wives and their kids. There were the people we had just bought the house from. There was that couple we had become friendly with during our holidays in St Rémy – they ran our favourite restaurant. And of course, there was the *Notaire*, accompanied by his impressive moustache.

It was to be the first and last in a long career of parties at which we were the only English people present. No-one knew anyone else. Stiff little clumps of people stood around our kitchen and salon, muttering among themselves and covertly examining our furnishings. The party was going to be a disaster. And then our three guests of honour came to the rescue: *Rouge, Blanc* and *Pastis*.

Eyes brightened. Voices rose. Laughter made itself heard. By the end of the evening Richard, our restaurant friend, had his arms around the *Notaire* and they were bellowing, tunelessly but with great enthusiasm, the Georges Brassens song *"Les Copins d'Abord"*.

Jeanne the estate agent's wife was dancing, all alone in the middle of the floor, eyes closed, swaying to music only she could hear. Her son, aged five, was curled up on the sofa, fast asleep with a strangle-hold on next door's shih-tsu.

At some point in the evening Himself made his excuses and fled. Dizzy with wine and translating I saw him go with some relief. By the time the last guests departed I was quite relieved to see them go, too. It was four a.m. and our entry onto the social scene of Morbignan la Crèbe had been a triumph.

'Allo 'allo!

It was the morning after. No special reason to get up, and I was smugly allowing myself a duvet day. So I was lying there peacefully, reviewing last night's triumphs and planning how I could bribe, cajole or threaten Patrick into going to get the breakfast croissant. After all, he had only been up until two the night before, while I didn't stagger into bed until after four. It was, I reasoned, his turn.

The next thing I knew, I was bolt upright in bed, whimpering 'What on earth was that?' Out of nowhere a voice was yelling in my ear. A woman's voice. A particularly strident woman's voice. *'Allo, 'allo!* she cried. It seemed to be coming from the vicinity of the church. 'This is it,' I thought. 'All those jokes, and it turns out God really *is* a woman, and she is calling me to account for my sins.'

But no, my hour had not yet come. What we later discovered was that *'Allo! 'Allo!* is the town crier. Ironically, we actually lived in the town crier's house: the *tambour*, who in olden times had marched round the medieval streets of the village with his drum, announcing that Madame Untel had lost her poodle; the bakery would close at noon for the *jour férié;* would residents please refrain from emptying their chamber pots in the gutter before 9 a.m. and, by the way, it was three o'clock and, on the whole, all was well.

Long gone was the *tambour*. In his place, *'Allo! 'Allo* resided atop the church in a gigantic pair of loudspeakers. In later years she (it was usually she) took to announcing her delivery with a blare of Occitan music, but at the time of our first introduction we would only be warned of the impending blast by a sort of pregnant stillness, followed by a semi-inaudible gulp.

Lost dogs, found keys, someone required urgently at the *Mairie*, the latest wild debauch offered by *Le Club du Troisième Age* - how would we have known about such things if *'Allo! 'Allo!* were not there to keep us informed?

Market day was when *'Allo! 'Allo!* really came into her own.. Morbignan has had a Wednesday market ever since the 14th century, by decree of the Bishops of Béziers no less. Sometimes as many as five or six stalls congregate in the square: the butcher, the florist, the greengrocer and occasionally, improbably, a stall selling dubious antiques run by Tiphaine, our local tame bohemian.

The shellfish man from Bouzigues visited the village of a Thursday, the chimney sweep arrived periodically and if we were really lucky we got a visit from Jo-Jo and his pizza van. And *'Allo! 'Allo!* was on hand to tell you all about it.

'Allo! Allo' she would cry gaily at some unearthly hour on market day. *'La poissonnière du Grau d'Agde est arrivée sur la place. AVEC...'* and here she launched into an interminable recitation of everything - but *everything* - the fishmonger had on her stall that day. *'Thon, raie, sole, baudroie, morue, encornets...'* It certainly did wonders for my restaurant French.

And of course it wasn't just the fishmonger. There was the aforementioned butcher, the fruit and veg man and the stall selling ladies' knickers *á des prix intéressants.* Each and every one of their wares had to be lovingly detailed, or else. *Une visite s'impose.*

And just when it seemed to be over, just when you thought it safe to take your fingers out of your ears, '*JE REPETE*,' she would say.

And she did.

Entente cordiale

They didn't speak to us, our English neighbours. Oh, they offered a polite *bonjour* if we met in the street, with all parties pretending not to know the other was English. They smiled thinly when our paths crossed. But they didn't mingle.

And quite right and proper, we thought. They didn't come here to be little Englanders, and neither did we. Like almost all the English people who come to the Languedoc to live, or to spend as much time as possible in our *maisons secondaires*, we were going to be more French than the French. We were going to live the French lifestyle, enjoy the French culture, and above all entertain French friends.

It wasn't difficult, at first. Twenty-odd years ago, when we opted for the Languedoc Roussillon as our French hideaway, it was largely undiscovered. We were among the first English people to settle in our village.

One of our predecessors, oddly enough, was the dishevelled Englishman who had accosted us, all those months ago, in the café in St Rémy. We'd almost forgotten about him, and I am anyway terrible at remembering faces, so it is not surprising that on our second encounter I had no idea who he was. Come to think of it, the exuberant manner and bristling Astérix moustache should have given me a clue, but there it is.

Astérix and his French wife had opened a restaurant, coincidentally, up on the hill above the very village where we had come to live. The day came when

56

we trotted up to make a reservation for the following evening. *'Bonjour, Monsieur,'* I greeted him politely, and launched into my mission – in French He replied in kind. Then – you could see the realisation dawn on both our faces. This person may speak French but he (she) is not French. That's when Himself piped up. 'Hello, Bash,' he remarked pleasantly. 'You see, we got here after all.'

Loud exclamations of delight and mutual recognition ensued. Then his sister appeared with mint tea. I knew I had come to the right place.

However, this select band of English was not to stay select for much longer. The Dordogne had become over-full and over-expensive and the British were on the march, looking for a new region to colonise. Eventually, inevitably, they came to our village. And, equally inevitably, they were going to be French.

Of course, it doesn't quite work that way, does it? We've all been to those parties where the majority of invitees are English and there, in the corner, stands the inevitable little bewildered clump of French guests. The butcher, the baker, the candlestick maker. Huddled together, discussing the events of the village, laughing up their sleeves at the silly English who are so desperate to integrate that they will invite anyone – but anyone – French. 'Oh yes,' the hosts chorus in blasé manner. 'Of course Jean-Thomas and Jean-Richard and Jean-Henri were at the party. They are DEAR friends...'

And the French came to our homes agog, eager to see what the foolish English had done next. Three-piece suites? Why, the old hard kitchen chairs serve perfectly well. Lamps in every corner? *Maman* managed fine for 80 years with the single 40-watt light bulb in the kitchen ceiling.

But this is not real integration. That takes a lot longer, and it's not just a question of language. Even if you speak good French, can rattle away with the best of them when you find yourselves in the queue at the *boulangerie*, the French just like to take their time. If you want to integrate, you have to do it at the locals' pace, not your own.

French manners are different from ours. You must greet your neighbours in the street, and a polite '*M'sieurs-Dames*' is de rigueur when you enter the post office or the *épicerie*. Beware: this does not mean you are bosom chums. There is a stately progression to such things. The obligatory *M'sieurs-Dames* means nothing. The nod in the street means nothing. The most important first step is the handshake.

Take the case of our neighbour Josiane – or Mighty Mouse, as we called her. She astonished us by introducing herself by her first name, instead of the more usual Madame Untel. Obviously we'd cracked it – any day now we'd be popping next door for cosy cups of coffee.

Not so. She and her big, looming, lugubrious husband Gérard remained smiling but distant. Until the day, some five years after the initial introduction, when we arrived on holiday from the UK. I should explain we call Josiane Mighty Mouse because she is small, frighteningly energetic and into everything. Whatever you're doing, Mighty Mouse will be there.

And so it was no surprise to find MM in the street, ostensibly watering her plants, as we drew up. What astonished us was what came next. 'You're back' she exclaimed   'How-are-you-did-you-have-a–good-trip-what-was-the-weather-like-how-long-are-you-staying-GÉRARD!!'   The last word on a positive bellow.

Gérard obediently ambled up. 'Now come and shake hands with these nice people,' she commanded, or the French equivalent thereof.

This was the breakthrough. In due time the handshake became a kiss (or *bisou*), and the longer we spent in the village the more handshakes (graduating to *bisous*) became the standard way of saluting our French friends. It wasn't too long before it took fully twenty minutes to greet everyone in the café (including *bisous* to the owner, his wife, his dad, his mum, his kids and his cat) – and woe betide us if we missed anyone out. The French who attended our parties were friends, not trophies.

And then, suddenly, it became OK to have English friends. After all, it's natural to want to chat in your own language some of the time.

I well remember the day those new English people moved into the village. I bumped into her in the *tabac* and introduced myself. Suggested she and her husband might like to pop in for an *apéro* once they were settled. She smiled politely – if a trifle nervously. 'Oh dear, here come the Little Englanders,' I could hear her thinking. 'You'll learn,' I told her silently.

As she is spoke

As we settled into our new summer home, anxious to get on with the neighbours and be accepted as soon as possible, I relied on one important fact. I spoke the language. Himself could get by with a charming shrug; I taught him to say '*Pardon Madame (Monsieur), je ne parle pas francais*' which he delivered with such aplomb that sometimes, to his horror, the response was a flood of rapid-fire French.

The French, we soon discovered, had much the same attitude to foreigners as, to my shame, we English do: speak loudly enough and the quaint Englishman will surely understand you.

My case was different. I had, after all, studied at a French school, taken French as part of my degree. Surely I would have no problems communicating? Alas, my confidence was misplaced. Talk to the *fonctionnaires* in the town hall, no problem. Discuss the weather with our venerable mayor in the café, no problem. But converse with my excitable neighbour or follow the thread of a lively discussion late in the evening, when the wine had flowed freely, and I was little better off than my hapless husband. Somehow the vocabulary I had acquired bore no resemblance to the language as she was spoke in the village.

For example, there is absolutely no hard-and-fast way of saying 'good evening' in French. Up to about, say, 4 p.m. there is a perfectly acceptable way to greet your friends and neighbours: *bonjour*. And if someone is toddling off to bed you can wish them *bonne nuit* and be fairly sure of getting it right. But 'good evening'? Forget it. You say *bonjour*, they say *bonsoir*. You say *bonsoir* and they say... guess what?

You might think that that the choice between *bonjour* and *bonsoir* is an individual one, and that each person has an interior clock which tells him when to switch over. Not so. My suspicion is that the whole thing is a gigantic tease; after all, it's practically a French national sport - making fun of the English.

One evening, soon after our arrival in the village, Himself and I were outside the *boulangerie* waiting for it to open and supply our evening *baguette*. One of our neighbours joined us, and Himself greeted her politely: '*Bonjour, Madame.*' '*Bonsoir,*' she replied with a kind, if rather pitying, smile. I am not slow on the uptake. '*Bonsoir Madame,*' I said smugly. '*Bonjour,*' she replied with a kind, if rather pitying, smile. *Mince*!

Mince?   No, it's not a craving for ground beef, nor an obsession with slimming. It's just one of those little expressions that our Gallic cousins slip in to the conversation, which no amount of dictionary thumbing can explain. In this case, *mince*, said with feeling, is a euphemism for the more earthy *m*rde*!

Other words come to mind. *Nickel* for example – and if you are English you should pronounce it neek-ell with enormous aplomb to avoid sounding silly – means spotlessly clean.

If you want to express approval you have to know when to say *génial* and when *impeccable* – a tricky one, that. You greet your close friends with *salut* and leave them with *ciao* (or the now-fashionable *baïe*, pronounced bye-eee). These friends are of course your *copins*, but beware of *copine* if you are a man (also known as a *mec*) because it could also mean your girlfriend.

Then of course there's *c'est pas évident*. Now this one really does not translate. For years my friends have been slipping the words in seemingly at random during otherwise perfectly comprehensible conversations. 'But what does it mean?' I would wail with increasing frustration. Nobody could, or would, explain. Then one day, as if on the road to Damascus, it came to me. I'd heard it in so many contexts that it somehow osmosed into my brain. I can use it with the best of them now, and get it right every time. '*C'est pas évident*' I cry, perhaps rather more often than strictly necessary. What does it mean? Well, to be honest, I've no idea.

Even more disconcerting is the way French expressions commonly used by the English completely baffle the French. Came the day we decided to give a party. The generally accepted method of inviting people was to put the word about, usually in the bar, but this, we had discovered, could lead to complications. Instead, I decided to be different and actually write formal invitations.

Then it occurred to me: whereas most of our English friends spoke or at least understood quite a lot of French, our French friends spoke and understood virtually no English. So I wrote the invitations in French and took them to a friend of mine, a retired *Lycée prof,* to check I had got the grammar right. He read the invitation through, corrected one mistake and told me the rest was fine, but 'What is this RSVP?' he wanted to know. Was he kidding? No – he was in earnest. '*Répondez s'il vous plait,*' I explained. 'You will have to explain it,' he warned. 'In France we don't know what this means.'

Of course both the English and French languages have their share of words with widely different meanings. That *baguette*, for instance, could also be found in the local *Bricomarché*, in which case it would be a long piece of plastic beading much beloved of plumbers and tilers. On the other hand, it's quite acceptable to ask for a *bâtard* in the *boulangerie*. And as for *baiser* – well, best not even go there.

Last but by no means is the splendid, immensely useful *alors?* There's a conversation-filler if you like. Need a word? Stuck for a riposte? *Alors?* will do nicely. And one glorious day I was able to use this delightful word to magnificent effect.

Patrick and I had acquired a small boat, which we moored at a local harbour. Small boats, it turns out, have one big drawback: the outboard engine. A recalcitrant piece of machinery if ever there was one. The theory is that you feed it some two-stroke fuel, then you pull the cord and - vroom! - It roars into life and you can set off on your cruise up the coast.

That is the theory. The practice is somewhat different. On that never to be forgotten day, Himself was doing battle as usual. He tugged on the cord. Nothing. He tugged harder. Mulish silence. Was the fuel tank full? It was. Was the petrol cock open? It was.

To the local youths idling on the harbour wall, here was divine comedy. They snorted, they chortled, they pointed. Growing bolder with every minute, they approached. Their joy escalated with every fruitless tug Himself, increasingly red-faced, inflicted on the boat's starter cord. Soon they were clutching their bellies with glee, shouting derision, smug in the knowledge that we had no idea what they were saying.

I had had enough. When I am angry, I am quiet, reasonable. Did they, I enquired calmly in French, perhaps speak English? Rather taken aback, they muttered '*Non.*'

Did they, I wondered, know anything about engines? A furious shaking of the heads.

Could they, I pursued, help us in any way? Answer came there none.

I drew myself up to my full height. I stared at them contemptuously. I gave the most elaborate, the most Gallic of shrugs. '*Alors?*' I enquired.

It was my finest hour.

Clock and bells

No-one who has ever spent any time in France will be surprised to learn that our house stood opposite the church. After all, it was on *La Rue de l'Eglise*, and the French are nothing if not literal. Put a hotel opposite a station and it is, inevitably, *L'Hôtel de la Gare*. Look for the post office and you can be sure of finding it on *La Rue de la Poste*.

Our church was old, which was about all you could say for it. Picturesque it wasn't, with its squat tower, blanked-out windows and patchwork of grubby *crépis* (plaster) where the stones had crumbled away. Many years later an energetic new mayor authorised major repair works. After eighteen months the newly refurbished church stood proudly in the newly cobbled square, with pots of geraniums and sheltered seating for the old folks. Sadly, though, the character of the old edifice was lost, and the open platform at the top of the bell tower, now enclosed, denied our local barn owl her roosting place. The nights were more peaceful without the eldritch shrieks of her young, but somehow sadder.

But all this was to come. What we very soon learned was that the church was not silent. We became acquainted with *'Allo 'allo* very early on in the proceedings, next we had to come to grips with the striking of the clock.

Under normal circumstances it struck every hour on the hour, give or take five minutes or so, and then two minutes later it struck again. This was surprisingly useful because by the time you had registered that the hour was striking it was generally too late to count the bongs.

Unless, of course, you woke in the night. The clock also struck once on the half hour and whatever time of night you woke, sure as eggs is eggs the next time the clock struck it would be a single bong. 'Oh, right,' you'd think. 'It's one o'clock. Or maybe it's half past. But half past WHAT??' And, vowing to stay awake until the hour struck, you'd drift off peacefully to sleep again.

Friends who came to stay were less than entranced. Our guest room faced the church directly: there was no escaping the noise. And noise it was: you couldn't call the chiming of our clock melodious at the best of times, but sometimes the bong would get swallowed up and all we got was a kind of strangled clanking. Himself invariably seized the opportunity to trot out his Joke. 'Oh, it's six o'clack' he'd exclaim to anyone who would listen.

Like any small village, ours had its sounds, sounds that made it uniquely Morbignan. Les Dawson and her poodle for instance. Yes, *her* poodle. One of our good ol' girls was the spit and image of the late comedian, toothless mouth set in a permanent scowl, small eyes peering suspiciously at the world. Les Dawson walked her poodle every night at ten. And every night the same scenario was enacted. *Bébé,* as the unfortunate creature was called, would make a bid for freedom. And every night, screeching across the rooftops, came the anguished cry of '*Bébé! Bébé!*'

When we got to know her, we discovered that 'Les Dawson' was actually charming. She would always stop for a sedate chat, invariably about the weather. '*Il fait beau.*' '*Il y a du vent*'. And in late summer she was occasionally to be found on my doorstep with an offering of wasp-pitted quinces or misshapen tomatoes from her garden.

The demon clarinettist was another old friend. For years after we first came to the village we would hear him doing his scales and exercises. Do mi sol mi sol mi sol… do re mi fa sol… Came the day when – jubilation! – the demon clarinettist learned a tune. Disconcertingly, it was "The Eton Boating Song".

There was no such thing as a peaceful lie-in in Morbignan. To begin with there was the rubbish truck which clanked up the street on Tuesday, Friday and Saturday, reversing with ear-splitting beeps round our narrow streets. Wednesday of course was Market Day, and *'Allo 'Allo* got into her stride well before 9 a.m., to tell us what the fishmonger had in store.

On Sundays we had the occasional Mass, the bell clanging dolefully to call the faithful to prayer, never mind last night's excesses and this morning's hangover. Mondays and Thursdays were relatively peaceful, apart from the neighbour's trucks which rumbled into life around 6 a.m. on most weekdays, taking him and his wife off to their jobs as market traders.

Of course, we heard none of it. Seasoned residents that we were, we effortlessly tuned out the church clock, the dog owners, the dustbin men, the local musicians. Until the day the clock fell silent. This was, actually, quite a regular occurrence. The mechanism was old, and every now and again it gave up entirely. What was strange was how much we missed it.

I once heard a story, probably apocryphal, about a lighthouse keeper somewhere on a rocky and turbulent shore of America. Every night for thirty years the lighthouse's siren would bellow mournfully every two minutes across the waves to warn ships of danger. And every night the lighthouse keeper slept peacefully in his bed. Until, one night, the mechanism failed and the siren did not go off. The lighthouse man sat up in his bed in alarm, crying 'What was that?'

I knew exactly how he felt.

Fur and feathers (and a few extra legs)

Once we had got used to the human and mechanical sounds of the village, we began to notice other noises, many of them made by birds of one type or another.

Most noticeable were the swifts – or swallows? – or martins? – which between April and September wheeled incessantly round the housetops. Imagine if you will a gang of small boys of five or six or seven, congregating on the corner with proud new Christmas bicycles. They gather, they chatter, then suddenly WHEEE! They're off, pedalling furiously, shrieking, laughing, swooping down the street and round the corner. Imagine that, and you've got our feathered visitors dead to rights.

Gulliver was one such, but his story comes later.

The Scops Owl was another visitor. For years this creature tantalised us with its cry - 'Bip... bip.... bip' - coming from the church tower, so regular and so monotonous that I was long convinced that it was something mechanical. Perhaps some un-oiled cog of the church clock? Knowledgeable friends assured us that it was an owl. Recourse to the bird book suggested, by a process of elimination, that it was a Scops owl.

More melodious was the nightingale. To our huge delight he (or she) sang the summer away for several years running, a voice we never tired of.

Then there was the Velcro bird. One summer it drove us mad with its two-tiered cry: a musical warble followed by a harsh 'kkkkhhhh.' It sounded exactly like two pieces of Velcro being ripped apart. I pestered ornithologicallyminded friends to tell me what it was; I even taped the little beast and once, just once, caught sight of it. Unfortunately it was what is known by the cognoscenti as an LBJ (Little Brown Job) so no identification was possible.

The following year there was no sign of the Velcro bird. On the other hand, we were caught out dozens of times by the sound of our front gate squeaking when there was no-one there. I suspected that the LBJ was a mimic.

The bats and lizards enchanted us every year. On the long summer evenings we'd sit out with a glass of wine waiting for that magical moment the French call *l'heure bleue*, when the shrieking birds had finally settled and the first pipistrelles fluttered out into the blue dusk. It became a point of honour to spot the first one.

After the scorch of noonday, when the sun at last began to relent, Sid would make his appearance. Sid was the generic name we gave to the lizards – all of them – with whom we were privileged to share our terrace during the summer months.

Over the years we came to know quite a bit about Sid. For example, his addiction to soft fruit. We got into the habit of leaving a piece of peach, strawberry or grape on the wall where Sid was wont to sun himself. Amazingly, one minute there were no lizards to be seen, a grape later and there were half a dozen circling the offering, snarling at each other (as we supposed from their body language) and making little darts at the fruit.

These were tiny lizards – the oldest and biggest no more than six or eight centimetres long – and we thought they were very cute indeed. Then, when I was experimenting with a video camera, I took a close-up shot. Suddenly these enormous jaws came into view and clamped with vicious intent on a piece of peach. Here was Tyrannosaurus Rex in miniature.

Out in the countryside it was a different story. Lizards lurked in the *garrigue*, lizards half a metre or more in length, lizards reputed to have a very nasty bite. These were shy creatures, rarely seen apart from a tail whisking out of sight as you rounded a bend in the road. On just one occasion though, as we drew into the street after a foray to the supermarket, we saw one of these beasts climbing our front steps. And I do mean climbing: it was so big that the height of the stairs presented no problem as it steadily made its way up towards the front door.

We both leapt out of the car in hot pursuit. I'm not sure exactly what we thought we were going to do – certainly not tackle it, if we had any sense. But the problem never presented itself: the lizard reached the terrace and simply disappeared. To this day we don't know what happened to it.

Birds, bats, lizards, all combined to make the long summer days and nights an enchantment, but other creatures less welcome lurked at the corners of our lives. I have to admit I do have a kind of sympathy with the rebellious creatures of Animal Farm. Four legs good, yes. Two legs bad? Well, not always. Six legs - or more? That's where I draw the line.

I was prepared for spiders, of course, when we moved into our Midi home. But nobody told me about scorpions. Scorpions are things you get in Africa, aren't they? Great black things a foot long with a sting that can stun an elephant. Surely not in the friendly south of France?

Until the day, or should I say the night, when I woke up and just knew I wasn't going to go back to sleep. It was a hot, hot summer night so I was wearing, er, not a lot. And when you switch on the light and there on the white wall is the biggest, blackest, evillest creepy crawly you ever imagined, and you haven't even the protection of a pair of socks, you do feel a tad vulnerable.

I wakened Patrick by the time-honoured method: 'Are you awake?' I hissed. And then, in the way of wives immemorial, I sweetly suggested 'Well, deal with THAT!'

I got a lot more laid-back in time. I learned to take scorpions in my stride, and preferred to capture them in a glass and put them outside, rather than send them prematurely to meet their maker. But one creature I could not, would not come to terms with was that long, hairy, multi-legged, evil-sting-equipped thing, the local centipede. Even today I'm even too afraid to squash them, let alone get near enough to trap them under a glass. Those, I'm afraid, take their chances in the next world – once I have summoned up enough courage to scream for help.

Manger, manger glorieux

August. A damp, depressing London August. We had been back two weeks from our second glorious holiday in the Morbignan house. My father had come to dinner, to hear the tale of our latest exploits. As we settled down to our *Tarte Tatin* – the cheese, *naturellement*, had come first - he shot me a dubious look over his spectacles.

'But what do you actually *do*, down there in the south of France?'

My father was American, Jewish, hard-headed. His idea of a holiday was to shoehorn in as many sights as could be crammed into a week or a fortnight. To him, the rationale for buying a property was its investment value. Lollygagging, as we call it, was a closed book to him.

'Well,' I answered slowly, knowing how he would react, 'we do spend a lot of time eating.'

There was a pause. Then, simultaneously, we burst out laughing.

But it got me thinking. We'd been visiting the Languedoc for several years by then, and were beginning to come to grips with the lifestyle. Food in France is, if you'll pardon the pun, an entirely different kettle of fish. To say 'we spend a lot of time eating' does not carry the same sense of urgency, you might even say gluttony, that it holds in our colder climes. Lingering late into the evening, even over a meal as simple as bread and cheese, is only paying your dues.

The French respect food, in a way that we do not. Take the words '*Bon appétit*.' Quite untranslatable. 'Good

Appetite' means nothing (and sounds faintly Germanic) while 'Enjoy your meal' just doesn't cut it. Yet *politesse oblige*, as you pass someone's table in a restaurant, to utter the phrase. When it's said to you - or to me at any rate - you feel a little glow of comradeship: we are sharing the love, sharing the respect.

And the French are not the slightest bit shy about it. I still remember, with a touch of hysteria, the day we were sitting in a favourite roadside picnic spot, feasting like royalty on *saucisson* and *fromage de chèvre*, fragrant olives and walnut bread. A Land Rover slid to a stop nearby and the driver hopped out. '*Bon appétit*' he called, and disappeared into the bushes for a pee. No Englishman I have ever met would call attention to himself with such cheerful insouciance while bound on such an intimate mission.

Then there's the lunch hour. In England it's a strict hour, if you're lucky. At the top of the corporate ladder you may find the fat cats lunching at leisure in their clubs, although that's more a myth than a reality these days. But for the less exalted - and especially middle management - a quick sandwich at their desks is a clear bid for brownie points.

Not so in France. *L'heure du repas* – or *l'heure du paing et du ving* as we like to call it, in honour of both the local accent and the local meal - is likely to extend to two hours; and this applies to all, from the lowliest shop assistant or office minion right up to the chief executive herself. Afterwards, the workers return refreshed and relaxed to renew their attack on the day's labours.

And then there's the question of where this feast takes place. Take a bunch of men in an English office. One o'clock rolls round and they head for the pub. And while they may shovel an unregarded pork pie into their mouths for sustenance, the main business of the hour is liquid.

Their French counterparts will gather at a local café or small neighbourhood restaurant. There won't be an extensive menu; it may be a case of 'You'll eat what we've got.' But it will be proper food, properly cooked and properly served at a table, with certainly an entrée and a main dish and often a dessert and/or coffee - and it will be treated with due regard. The French on the whole don't tolerate shoddy food, and will vote with their feet if it is not up to standard.

Things are no different on the road. If you're driving in France and the hands of the clock are creeping towards lunch, keep your eyes open for the café or service station with the largest collection of lorries outside. Good plain food and plenty of it will be the order of the day. French truck drivers are no fools where their stomachs are concerned.

Even when it comes to the humble picnic, the French have a certain flair. There was the day when, on the road to somewhere or other, we stopped in a leafy *aire* for a spot of lunch. Four men who I can only imagine were commercial travellers had had the same idea. Their suit trousers were pressed. Their suit jackets were carefully hung over the back of their picnic chairs, the sleeves of their immaculate white shirts neatly rolled up.

There was a checked cloth on the table. Plates, glasses and cutlery were set out, a *baguette* sat on a bread board and there was a selection of cheese and *charcuterie* on the table before them. They looked so happy, relaxed and carefree that I just couldn't resist.

'*Bon appétit, Messieurs*!' I called out.

My father is long gone now. But every time we sit down to a slow, self-indulgent Languedoc meal, as the sun sinks behind the olive trees and the first bats flutter out into the blue dusk, I find myself explaining it to him all over again. In France, you spend a lot of time eating.

The summer of the cat

'I saw Pouchkine today,' I remarked, setting down my shopping bag of strawberries and asparagus on the kitchen floor. 'He was sitting on an elephant.' My husband gave me the same look that, a summer ago, I had given him when one afternoon he had suddenly announced 'There's a cat in here.'

As it turned out, neither of us was either mad or hallucinating. I really had seen Pouchkine – a furry green-eyed butterball of a cat – sitting on the stone elephant which topped my neighbour's gatepost. And he really had wandered into our lives, unannounced, the summer before. It was on a particularly hot afternoon. Chased inside by the sun, we had withdrawn to the cool of the kitchen and were sipping a last glass of wine, contemplating siestas. Suddenly, 'There's a cat in here,' said Himself.

'Of course there is, dear,' I soothed, wondering if that last glass of *rosé* had really been such a good idea. Boot-faced, Himself pointed to the shadiest corner of the room. There indeed was Pouchkine, curled up and obviously intending to stay. The dance had begun.

And how we danced to his tune, all that summer. Pouchkine had adopted us. He had a perfectly good home of his own, with Mme Bretel, three houses down from us, and judging by his girth he didn't go short, but the French are pragmatic about their pets. They feed and look after them, but they don't dote. All the animals of the village knew that if you wanted a really *good* billet, with humans falling over themselves to indulge your every whim, find an English family.

Our first mistake was to give him a name. We called him, as many cats are called, Pushkin; but in deference to the local accent it soon became Pouchkine – pronounced poosh-keen with as heavy an Occitan inflexion as you could manage. As soon as the cat heard this outlandish collection of syllables and realised it referred to him, he knew he had us. Thereafter, he ruled us with a steely determination.

By day, Pouchkine came and went as he chose. We never let him stay the night, though. When it came time for sleep we would put him, protesting, out of the door, to go about his lawful business or find his legitimate bed. We didn't want to get into any squabbles with an indignant neighbour.

Perhaps what then ensued was Pouchkine's idea of revenge. Our day started at 6 a.m. Never mind if you'd been up late the night before, gossiping with friends on the terrace or whooping it up at the local *café concert,* and fancied a lie-in: at six sharp Pouchkine was there on the doorstep.

'Waaow?' Silence. We'd hold our breath, hoping we'd misheard. Then: 'Waaow? *Waaow?'*

Again, silence, but it was not to last. Just as we were drifting off back to sleep: 'Waaow? Waaow? WAA-ow?' By then I'd be awake, lying tense and cursing my own *Englishness:* I knew I was going to give in.

'WAAOW! WAAOW! *WAAOW!* (I can keep this up forever) WAAA-OW! WAAA-OW! *WAAAAA-OW! WAAA...'*

'Oh, all RIGHT.' I'd get out of bed (yes, it was usually me) and stagger downstairs. When I opened the front door there he sat, as if wondering what took me so long. 'Where's my milk, then?'

Of course, as you've probably guessed, we enjoyed it. How pleasant to while away the evening in idle talk, with a fat furry grey lump sitting purring on one of our laps. Although we were both animal lovers we didn't – then – have one of our own. Pouchkine made a nice surrogate.

The summer passed, as summer will. It was time to go home. 'What will happen to Pouchkine?' I fretted. I needn't have worried. Back in the Languedoc the following summer, I saw Pouchkine. He was sitting on an elephant. I approached with trepidation, holding out coaxing fingers for his favourite scratch behind the ear. Flinching back as though I had proffered hot coals, he gazed at me disdainfully down his nose. 'You left me,' his green-eyed stare reproached me. 'Left me here to starve.'

Starve! He was, if anything, fatter than ever. 'But we had to go back to England,' I pleaded. 'We couldn't have taken you with us: you would have hated it. Besides,' I hesitated, seeking the most diplomatic form of words, 'besides, you don't *appear* to be starving. Madame Bretel obviously keeps you well fed. In fact, you seem remarkably well-covered to me.'

I hadn't chosen my words carefully enough. Pouchkine leapt from the elephant and stalked off, his tail stiff with offence. I hung my head.

Such is the tyranny of cats.

The end of the world as we knew it

Friday 18th July 2003 was just like any sleepy summer day in Morbignan. Of course, it was hot. We were going through what the French call *La Canicule* that year – a devastating heatwave that killed thousands of people across Europe. We very soon learned that the only way to get anything done was to get up at 6 a.m., or even earlier if possible, and go about our business until 10:30 and then retire to whatever shelter we could find until around 7:30 that evening.

Whoever had built our house, some 200 years earlier, knew all about heat waves. The stone walls were two feet thick and after we had insulated the roof space – to the great hilarity of the builder whom we asked to do it – the house was as cool as it was possible to be.

On that Friday we had braved the scorching temperatures to cross the square and have lunch at the café. Jean-Paul had installed air conditioning the year before, which did wonders for business. We had finished our *salade de chèvre* and our *iles flottantes* and were lingering over a coffee, trying to summon up the energy for the dash home, when Simon came into view with a determined glint in his eye.

Now Simon, an Englishman of some 40 years, was the *boute-en-train* – the mover and shaker of the village. Social occasions were his forte: New Year's Eve gatherings, Halloween parties, surprise birthday parties, Indian suppers at the bar - many of these wouldn't have happened without Simon to organise them. When I say organise, though, I don't actually mean rolling up his sleeves and getting down to it. Therein lay the rub: Simon was brilliant at coming up with ideas, and then leaving it to the rest of it to organise boring details like calculating how many kilos of sausages we'd need for a communal barbecue and did we have enough chairs if Marie-Paulle's six children all came along. We soon came to know that Simon's 'Why don't we...' – while a prelude to some undeniably novel and entertaining proposition – invariably meant 'Why don't you...'

I was in no mood for Simon. A lazy siesta and a book in the shade beckoned, and I knew that once Simon had launched into his latest project we would be stuck in the café for at least another hour.

'Quick!' I hissed to Himself, 'Let's make a move before he gets to our table.' Unfortunately we weren't quite quick enough. I was on my feet, gathering up my bag and sun hat and looking purposeful, but Himself was still savouring the last dregs of his coffee, sprawled comfortably on the hard café chair and looking good for a long natter. His loss, I thought, and pleading a migraine I made my excuses and left.

Two delicious hours passed. I was drowsing happily over my book on the terrace, reflecting smugly on my timely escape from the café, when I heard the kitchen door open. Horror of horrors, I heard Patrick talking. He'd brought Simon home to continue the conversation! I quickly pulled on a robe to cover my bikini, and a smile to cover my fury, and rushed into the kitchen. There stood Himself, alone. Or, when I took a second look, not quite alone. In his arms was a small brown and white bundle, which he proceeded to place gently on the floor. The bundle stirred, got to its feet and looked up at me with huge brown eyes.

It wasn't quite a puppy, but it wasn't fully grown either. Obviously lost, bewildered and rather frightened, it cautiously began to explore the kitchen. 'She's a stray,' Patrick explained. 'She came into the bar and Jean-Paul shooed her out again, but when I came outside she was still there, running around in the road. Lucien (one of the village good ol' boys, who adored dogs) said I'd better take her home or she would get run over.'

There was rather more to it than that, as I later discovered. Patrick is as soppy about dogs as anyone I know, and they adore him. He often says that they can see 'mug' tattooed on his forehead in dog-speak, and for all I know it's true. It seems that the little creature had taken one look at him, put her paws on his knee, gazed up at him adoringly with those big brown eyes – and that was that. As I now regularly explain to my friends, 'she's a French tart: she picked my husband up in a bar.'

Here I have to admit that I'm equally besotted about dogs. Himself and I had many a time discussed getting one, had had mature and sensible discussions on the subject and had come to the mature and sensible decision that as we were both working and travelling regularly, it wouldn't be fair to the animal or to us. We both feel strongly that taking on an animal is a major responsibility.

But the heart wants what the heart wants, and so when Himself said 'We'll keep her for tonight and take her to the animal shelter tomorrow' I should have realised that it wouldn't quite turn out like that. For a start, it was Friday, and the animal shelter wouldn't be open until Monday, so we she was ours for the weekend.

She was wearing a collar, though no tag, so we attached her to a piece of cord and set out into the village in search of a lead and some dog food, before calling in at the *Mairie* to announce her arrival. Perhaps 'Allo 'Alllo would summon up the little dog's owner.

Over the next two days we began to get acquainted. I made the fatal mistake of giving her a name. 'We can call her Perdita, because she was lost,' I said, 'or Perdi for short.' It was a joke, of course, or so I thought. Perdi (or Purdey, as she later became) quickly made herself at home. We soon learned that she was feisty, demanding and affectionate – and immensely greedy. Anything we put in front of her, she ate. Anything we didn't put in front of her, if it was edible, she stole.

Had she been neglected, underfed? Not a bit of it. She was sleek in her long brown and white coat, with ginger eyebrows and endearing hints of orange on her bum. Her tail was abbreviated, with an absurd tassel of white hair at the end of it – we came to call it her preposterous apostrophe. She was pretty, sociable and confident – friends came to coo and stayed to cuddle. What she was, we didn't know. Some kind of spaniel, we thought, though not exactly like any spaniel we had come across.

Monday came, and I was invited to have coffee with my friend Josiane. Could I, I asked her on the telephone, bring Purdey with me? '*Mais bien sûr!*' Leaving Patrick to enjoy his newspaper, we set out. Josiane had a pretty garden, with tall and shady fig trees, and we were enjoying a coffee and a gossip while Purdey made short work of a large bone my hostess had conjured from somewhere. Came a loud knocking at the door. Josiane went to answer it, and returned followed by Michael, another neighbour, looking flustered. 'You have to come home,' he said, 'Patrick sent me to fetch you: the dog's owner has turned up.'

I got home in a hurry, the dog leaping ahead of me in excitement. A small, energetic Frenchman was waving his arms about in our kitchen. It seemed that our furry visitor wasn't a stray after all. Insatiably curious, she had got bored sitting next to her master as he lunched and gossiped with his cronies, and wandered off to see what was what. We hadn't so much rescued her as kidnapped her.

On seeing her master the dog flattened her ears, lowered her preposterous stump of a tail and looked ashamed of herself. Himself just looked stricken. I decided to take matters in hand. I hesitated. I looked at Himself, I looked at the dog. Then I took a deep breath and spoke the words which, did I but know it, were to change our lives beyond all recognition. 'Monsieur,' I said, 'we like your dog. May we buy her from you?'

And that was the end of the world as we knew it.

THREE:
At Home
in the Pays
d'Oc

People do tend to look a bit startled when we explain that she was a kidnap.

A half-blood princess

Monsieur Ducros, as we came to know him, reflected for a second. 'Well,' he said at last, 'she is meant to be a hunting dog, but she is afraid of gun shots so I can't use her.'

This, we were to discover, was not unusual. The village was obsessed with hunting. Every weekend from September to March you were quite likely to walk into the bar and find a pile of twelve-bores sitting on the pool table. The routine was this: the good ol' boys would roll in from their labours in the vines and take their midday *pain et vin* before heading for the hills, 'loaded for bear'. The truth of it was, though, that they were by no means loaded for bear: those impressive guns were usually equipped with nothing more lethal than bird shot, which scattered far and wide and did relatively little damage. And this was just as well, because, fortified with rather more *vin* than *pain*, they were apt to fire off at anything that moved.

This could cause serious problems, such as when our neighbour Matthieu let fly at one of the local wild boar. A faceful of shot won't stop a boar, but it will make it seriously pissed off. Matthieu spent the rest of that afternoon up a tree, and was only rescued by chance when his son – known to everyone as P'tit Mat – came looking for his father with buckshot in his twelve-bore.

Usually, though, the hunters merely shot one another – not surprising since they all insisted on wearing camouflage gear – but their poor dogs often came in for a stray piece of flak, too. Many a dog was seen wandering round the village with half its nose missing. They weren't too keen on going hunting with their masters after that. Luckily the little dog sitting in our kitchen had her nose intact, but to this day she carries a scar on her upper lip which, I think, explains a lot.

To return to that Monday: I translated the conversation to Patrick, who had been hopping from foot to foot with impatience. Joy replaced consternation. Sensing something to her advantage was afoot, the dog jumped happily up at M. Ducros, who pulled her ears affectionately and told her to be good. Tanya she was, Purdey she became, and now rules our lives with a paw of iron.

Some thirteen years later, as we take our morning walk along the beach, we stop for a chat with other dog owners and naturally the question arises: 'Was she a stray?' People do tend to look a bit startled when we respond: 'No, she was a kidnap.' The next question, invariably, is 'What *is* she?'

When Purdey first wandered into our lives we knew she was a spaniel of some kind. The problem was, she didn't quite fit into any category of spaniel we had encountered before: too small for a springer, too slight for a cocker. Rather dismissively, the vet wrote *épagneule croisée* (spaniel cross) on her new identity card. Surely not, we thought. Our graceful, glossy-coated new friend with her fine bones and prancing gait couldn't possibly be a mongrel.

The question was resolved two weeks later when an American friend came to stay with us. Taking one look at the dog, who was sitting on his feet gazing adoringly at the biscuit in his hand, 'She's a Britney.' he announced with absolute certainty. We looked at each other doubtfully. The only Britney we knew was the pop star.

She was cute and popular, yes, but could she really have had a breed of dog named after her? It was, it seemed, a question of accent. Seeing our blank faces our friend explained that a Britney came from Britney, 'You know, in the west of France.' Then the penny dropped. 'Oh, you mean a Brittany,' I said rather tactlessly. 'That's what I said, isn't it?' he replied huffily.

A quick consultation of the dog breeds book confirmed it. The Brittany Spaniel – now just called a Brittany – is found in France and America but is rare in the UK. The classic version of the breed is orange and white, with softly rounded ears and smooth fur. There were plenty of those in the village, but Purdey looked nothing like them. She was mainly dark chocolate and cream, with apricot eyebrows and touches of the same colour round the face and on her bottom. Her fur was long and silky. She belonged to the rarer, tri-coloured version of the breed, but nonetheless she was a purebred Brittany, or so we thought.

But my husband had his doubts. There was a dog about the village. A leering, lolloping, handsome chap with a twinkle in his eye and a long plumy tail. A roguish fellow who might easily seduce a nicely brought-up young Brittany from the paths of virtue. Himself got it into his head that here was Purdey's true father. 'When you see them together,' he insisted, 'they have exactly the same walk. And when they finish their ablutions they both scrape their paws and growl in exactly the same way.'

I refused to believe it. To my mind Purdey was pure Brittany, and that was that. Her imperious ways and whim of iron had already earned her the title The Princess Purdey of Morbignan.

It was the dog's former owner himself who settled the matter. One day as we were walking by the river, a little white van drew alongside us and M. Ducros emerged. Purdey greeted him rapturously, eyes shining, stumpy tail wagging furiously. 'I have her mother here,' said M. Ducros. 'Perhaps you'd like to meet her.' He opened the back door of the van, and out jumped a classic Brittany spaniel. She was orange and white, with a smooth coat. Purdey greeted her politely, but with no apparent recognition.

Patrick regarded the two dogs thoughtfully. 'Tell me, Monsieur, was her father also a Brittany?' The old farmer's brow darkened. 'No,' he snapped, 'it was that dog you see round the village. He jumped over the fence...' I looked at Himself in dismay. 'Do you realise what this means?' I whispered. 'Purdey, our Perdita, is a Half-blood Princess. She must never know.'

Once in a while, now that we are back in England, we will take our morning walk along the beach and some frightfully pukka, county and kennel-club type will come up to us. 'Ah yes,' he will muse (it's invariably 'he'), 'you've got a Brittany there.' And he will look so pleased with himself for recognising the breed that we haven't the heart to correct him.

A Radical Re-think: The Purdey Factor

'Monsieur, we like your dog, may we buy her from you?'
What was I thinking?

Truth to tell, I wasn't thinking at all. My husband
and I had been bowled over by a pair of big brown eyes,
and had – without discussing, without considering –
plunged headlong and heedless into dog-ownership.

This was all the more ironic since only a week or
two earlier my neighbour Sharon and I had gone to coo
over some new-born puppies in the village. 'Careful,' I
warned her, as she seemed about to succumb, 'you're
letting yourself in for fifteen years of poop-scooping.'
Sharon did not succumb, but I could imagine the glee with
which she would throw my sensible words back at me
when I appeared with Purdey in tow.

This, though, was the least of our worries: the
problem was that in those days we still travelled regularly
between the UK and France. It was in the very early days
of the European pet passport scheme, and although it was
possible to take the dog with us, there was a stumbling
block. Purdey had been neither microchipped nor
inoculated against rabies. Both of these things are
obligatory before an animal can enter the UK. Simple, we
thought in our innocence. Down to the vet for a shot and a
chip, and away we go. We soon learned different. First
comes the microchip; a few days later the vet presents us
with her paperwork. She is on her way to becoming an
international traveller.

Before that can happen, though, there is the matter of the rabies vaccination. Although the UK had relaxed its rules about the import of animals, on this point it was firm: no entry was permissible until the shot had been administered, and 'taken'. What we hadn't realised was that, in those days, we would have to wait a full six months before Purdey could be deemed rabies-free.

By the time Purdey came into our lives Himself was easing towards early retirement, and I was running my own business which, with a bit of adjustment, could be carried out for the time being from the South of France. It was a matter of no great difficulty to arrange to stay on in Morbignan until after Christmas. By then she would be able to travel, and we would take her back home to the UK. We would, we thought, resume our old lives: living in London and holidaying, as often as possible, in Morbignan.

I have to say it was a bit of a shock to the system. In the past our winter visits had been limited to a couple of weeks at Christmas, when the weather was bright and cold or bright and mild, but above all bright. Slowly, things were changing: we were getting a lot more rain, and the dry crisp cold was giving way to an altogether murkier climate. That first winter with Purdey was a foretaste of things to come. But, with no other option, we gritted our teeth and got on with it.

Somehow we got through the slow months until it was time for our return to the UK. I have to admit I was looking forward to spending time in our centrally-heated flat, with the bright lights of London on my doorstep.

What we hadn't reckoned with was the Purdey factor. We lived at the time on the second floor of a block of flats, high on a hill in Cricklewood. For humans, the flat was comfortable, attractive and warm. For a little dog who a year ago had been living in a farmer's yard among her siblings, it was hell. She constantly roamed the flat looking for a way out, her eyes begging for the old familiar streets of Morbignan, the river walks, the gallops in the vines. How could we explain to her that every walk meant getting into the car and driving somewhere: the nearest park was three miles away.

We made shift as best we could, eventually finding a friendly football club which would allow her to romp round its field when it was not in use, but to her it wasn't the same thing at all. Then there were the inevitable late-night walks, usually undertaken by Himself, always on tarmac or pavement.

It became more and more clear that London living and a country dog didn't mix. It was time for a radical re-think. Now we sat down and had the long conversation which we should have had before ever embarking on this adventure.

As we saw it, we had three options. Return Purdey, regretfully, to M. Ducros. After a month or two she would have forgotten all about us, happily resuming her old ways, but we would be broken-hearted. Or we could leave London for good and become full-time expatriates. Out of the question. I am – or was then – a Londoner to my fingertips. My friends, my work, my amusements were all centred on the capital. I was baffled by the thought that anyone *could* live outside London.

And this only left one choice: Morbignan would become our place of residence more or less full-time, but we'd take trips back to the UK as often as we could manage, for work or for recreation. No way were we going to sell the London flat: it was my lifeline to what I thought of as civilisation. But yes, effectively, we were going to make our home in the Pays d'Oc.

Plaster under the bed

When we were looking for our house, we had one other stipulation for our friend Jean-Jacques the estate agent. In addition to having the required garage, terrace and *boulangerie*, the house must be in good repair. Patrick, remembering the travails of his London experience, was adamant on the subject. 'It's hard enough to keep tabs on the builder, the electrician and the plumber when you're just down the road,' he said. 'How can we be expected to do it from 800 miles away?' He had a point.

Luckily the house we had fallen in love with did not require any serious building work. I must admit we felt a tad smug about this when we listened to our friends' tales of woe. But that was back in the days when the Morbignan house was strictly for holidays. The kitchen was charming, but impractical. The loo was on the ground floor - a cold tramp down the stairs in the middle of the night. Our bedroom could only be accessed through the spare room.

All this was fun during the holiday months, not so much fun if we were going to be living there year-round. Changes would have to be made. And so it was that we prepared to face the trauma that so many of our ex-pat friends had already gone through: Having the Builders In. In fact, it was probably no more traumatic than anything our friends back home might experience, but with this difference: we had to do it all in French. Not just in the language – that would have been relatively easy – but in the French *modus operandi*, Languedoc-style.

When it came to builders in our village, P'tit Gui was the main man. He was already getting on in years when we first met him, and didn't do much hands-on work, but the *entreprise* was his, and he sent the work force in. P'tit Gui loved us to bits. He often dropped in just for a chat, and looked hurt when we tactfully suggested that we discuss the work in hand.

Henri was the plasterer and bricklayer. He was in his sixties, a wiry and astonishingly handsome little man with a big laugh and a personality to match. Getting to Henri was best done through P'tit Gui although, as Henri never tired of telling us, he didn't work for P'tit Gui. *Mais non*, he was just helping out as a favour.

Henri was an absolute master of his craft. His plasterwork was glass-smooth and his walls went up in no time - flat, straight and rock-solid - but neat he was not. When Henri got into his stride, it was wise to duck. He's working on the bathroom? There are flecks of plaster under the bed. He's building a wall downstairs? There are fragments of brick in the garden. When at six sharp he clocked off, assuring me he had tidied up behind him, I didn't need to go and look – I knew that wherever he had been working would look like Armageddon, only messier.

If you wanted a parquet floor, kitchen cabinet or window frame, Monsieur de St. Phalle was your man. Thierry, as he graciously allowed us to call him, was the neighbourhood carpenter. His work was exquisite and he was consequently much in demand but, by Midi standards, he was as reliable as they come.

One day, though, he failed to turn up as promised, so the next day Himself and I went to beard him in his sawdust-scented lair above the village. He looked at us mournfully with eyes the colour of ginger wine. 'I am so sorry I didn't come,' he apologised, 'I had to go to a funeral.' Thinking 'Oh yeah? Pull the other one,' we nonetheless made the proper noises. Thierry looked bemused by our condolences: 'No, you don't understand,' he said. 'I am also the undertaker.'

Like P'tit Gui, Thierry took a liking to us. It was rather a pitying liking, as of one who would say 'They're only English: they can't help it.' This was probably due to the Incident of the Airing Cupboard.

Contrary to popular belief, the Languedoc is not always hot and sunny. Every day is not a drying day, and when the weather decides to do damp and dismal, getting the sheets and towels aired can be difficult. We English understand the problem. *Midi* natives, brainwashed by their region's publicity, do not.

We explained to Jean-Jacques that what we wanted was a cupboard with a heater inside it, for storing household linens. He looked at us in incredulity. He asked us to repeat what we had said. He began to giggle. Then he howled. It was the funniest thing he'd ever heard. What a shining example to recount, over a *pastis*, of the folly of the English. He duly built the cupboard but thereafter never failed to greet us in the street with a joking enquiry as to its health. Why is it that the English seem to exist only to provide an endless source of innocent merriment for the French?

As builders went, ours were reliable. If they promised faithfully to get the job done they usually did so. In their own time, true. After much nagging, certainly. But they did actually build, and their work was good. Of course this was in itself a mixed blessing. Being reliable – Midi fashion – and delivering good work meant that they were swamped with commissions. And, being charming people, they just hated to disappoint…

For anyone contemplating the awful step of taking on a southern French work force, a few key phrases will come in useful. *'Oui'* means 'perhaps, but I'm not promising anything.' *'Certainement,'* or – worse – *'Sans faute'* means 'forget it.'

Other useful expressions are:

A deux heures	before five (probably)
Demain(g) (probably)	by the end of the week
Jeudi (probably)	by the end of the month
La semaine prochaine	never: by the time next week comes they will have forgotten all about you

There are tips and wrinkles when it comes to dealing with builders in the Midi. First of all, it's no good whatever being English about it. We English are so *polite*. We plead, cajole and thank effusively for service. If a builder turns up when he is expected we positively roll out the red carpet. Coffee? Croissants? Of *course* you can light up a Gauloise in my newly decorated, smoke-free-zone kitchen.

If, fired with indignation, we manage to pin down a builder and demand to know why he hasn't delivered what he promised, the slightest hint of tetchiness on his part will send us grovelling back into apology mode.

Now this won't do at all. My neighbour Josiane - Mighty Mouse - used to despair of me. She went to school with P'tit Gui, our local builder. She called him 'tu'. She exchanged *bisous* with him. And still she nagged and threatened, scolded and shrieked like a fishwife to get the job done. If he was more than 30 seconds late for an appointment she was on the phone, breathing brimstone.

And did she get results? Well, after a fashion. Probably rather more than we did, in the early, timorous days. But we had to learn: this was the Midi. And it was heartening to realise you didn't have to be English to suffer from The Builders.

As we became more experienced in the ways of the builder, we began to consider ourselves a match for him. There was a game which was popular among all of us *bonnes ménagères* – English and French alike. It was called *Cherchez le Maçon*. It went something like this. Marie Elizabeth lived opposite the café, her nets permanently a-twitch. Spotting P'tit Gui taking a morning coffee, she would instantly be on the phone to Josiane, who then popped next door to tell me. I would phone Helga, who lived a little way outside the village, and so it went on. The cry went up: 'P'tit Gui is in the village!' and suddenly Gui's peaceful *crème* would be rudely interrupted as half a dozen harpies descended on the café.

More subtle, and even more satisfying, was the game of 'Gotcha!' It went like this: say a good friend has actually managed to tie P'tit Gui to an appointment at 2 p.m. Because she is a mate, she tells a chosen few. We all descend at 1:50 and lurk in her kitchen. Of course, we know that P'tit Gui probably won't actually turn up until three o'clock at the earliest, but he has been known to wrong-foot us. Besides, she makes excellent coffee.

Eventually Gui turns up, an unsuspecting fly buzzing into the communal web. And -WHAM! - three or four determined spiders pounce. The look on his face makes the game worth the candle: outrage, mixed with a you-got-me-bang-to-rights sheepishness. And, of course, that roguish twinkle which was the reason we all put up with him.

Talking Rubbish

They were early that morning. A distant rumble heralded their arrival. It grew to thunder. Strange cries pierced the air. Perhaps because we had been out late the night before, they sounded louder than usual.

We huddled under the duvet, knowing what was coming. Ear-splitting mechanical beeps told us they were now going backwards. Next came the recriminations. 'Did you put the bin out?' 'No, I thought you did.' 'No, it was YOUR turn.' 'No, I walked the dog, and you said…' Once again the green (or yellow) bin would stand un-emptied and overflowing in the garage for another three days.

What was the source of the disturbance? The dustmen, of course, or *les poubellistes*, as I liked to call them. Their Wagnerian performance, and the attendant angst, became part of our lives. Three days a week, come rain come shine – but not of course on *jours fériés* – the Dustman Cameth.

It was not always thus. There were many buzzwords flying around in the late 1980s when we first went to spend our summers in Morbignan. 'Environment' wasn't one of them. Rubbish was just something you disposed of, landfill sites a fact of life. You might take your empties to a bottle bank, but those days of crippling shame when you make the mistake of throwing a piece of cardboard into the domestic rubbish bin were far in the future.

So our main concern, once we had settled in, was where and when to put out the *ordures ménagères*. Oh, said our neighbours, just put the rubbish out in the street on Mondays, Wednesdays and Fridays and it will be collected.

We might have known it wouldn't be as simple as that. To begin with, there were strict rules about *when* you could put it out. Not before nine o'clock the previous evening, we were told sternly, having transgressed. But the local dogs were unimpressed by curfew. Come nine o'clock they congregated merrily and did the round of the rubbish bags, leaving havoc and grapefruit skins in their wake.

This led to some ingenious solutions. Stroll through the village of an evening on the eve of collection, and you would see black plastic bags swinging from gateposts and terraces like misshapen felons from a gibbet.

A few years after this, we were told that rubbish would no longer be collected from our doorsteps. Now this might sound as if we were losing a valuable civic service, but in fact it was an improvement. Instead of having to remember to put the bins out, and living under the threat of having their contents strewn across our doorstep by enthusiastic local canines, we were in full charge. When your kitchen waste bin was full you simply took it to the nearby skip.

To sweeten the pill, it was announced that we would be issued with rubbish bags by a benevolent local council. Once a year, usually just after Christmas, the villagers would line up like paupers on Maundy Thursday to receive their allotted parcel of plastic bin liners. We were usually away at that time of year, and so missed out, but one memorable year we were actually at the house when 'Allo 'Allo announced that *les sacs de poubelle* would be distributed at *la mairie* today.

Gleefully we took our place in the queue. But what was this? Our bundle was paltry compared to that received by Mme Untel, next to me in line. I dared to protest – why were we not receiving our full allotment? 'Oh,' said the town clerk, with a smile both pitying and supercilious, 'but you are *maison secondaire.*'

Things went on in this fashion until a couple of years after we took up full-time residence. One dank and wet November night 'Allo 'Allo summoned the populace to come to the *Salle des Fêtes* to talk rubbish. No, it wasn't an invitation to attend a local council meeting, as more than one wag suggested. It was much more serious than that.

France, it seemed, had entered the age of the Environment. Henceforward we would be expected to recycle our rubbish. Shortly we would be issued with special bins, and told (you should forgive the expression) where to put them. Confusingly, the eco-bins would turn out to be yellow and the non-eco ones green. And should we dare to stray from the straight and narrow we would risk incurring the wrath of SICTOM – the *Syndicat Intercommunal de Collecte et Traitement des Ordures Ménagères.*

The French have their own endearing ways of doing things, so it was no surprise that this fairly simple step required a meeting lasting two hours followed by the issue of a 12-page booklet explaining the whole thing again. For the English among us, I'm afraid, it was more sitcom than SICTOM. Glances were exchanged. Smiles turned to giggles and giggles to guffaws, tactfully disguised as coughs and sneezes.

Not that we were against this development. Far from it. Most of us approved heartily of the recycling effort. We were already dutifully lugging our bottles to the bottle bank outside the post office, where the Good Ol' Boys dozed on a bench and begged us to leave any full ones with them.

What tickled us was the immense, Gallic seriousness of the whole operation. The amount of discussion it entailed. The endless newsletters and circulars that followed over the months, updating the Dos and Don'ts and giving progress reports on the recycling campaign.

Alas, the seriousness was mainly civic. The populace didn't give a hoot, as it turned out. I discovered this one Easter Saturday. It was never very clear in our part of the world what is and is not *férié* over Easter. I'd gone round the corner and seen no yellow bins, so had concluded that *Les Poubellistes* were not coming today. But then, as I strolled to the *boulangerie* I heard the rumble of distant wheels.

In a panic I rushed back and extricated the bin from its lair in the garage. I arrived in time to catch the men just as they were turning to leave. I explained that, as I had seen no yellow bins in the designated space, I had assumed they weren't coming. '*C'est normal,*' they said scornfully, '*Vous n'êtes pas sérieux dans ce village.*'

Cellar Wars

On the whole, we got on well with our neighbours. Josiane, of course, was a chum: we had many a natter on our front steps, shared many a glass of wine on our terrace or in the shade of her fig tree. Josiane knew all the local news: who was having an affair, whose kids had passed the Bac' with flying colours – if you wanted the latest gossip, Josiane was invaluable.

Others were just as friendly. After a year or two, having proved our credentials as *des gens correctes*, we couldn't so much as cross the little square to the post office without exchanging smiles, *bonjours*, handshakes and even the occasional *bisou* with our neighbours.

Madame Lacoste – owner of the unfortunate poodle Bébé – would bring me quinces in season and accept, with a certain reserve, a jar of the resultant chutney. Matthieu the plumber occasionally left a rabbit on the doorstep and then called round to tell me exactly how to cook it;

Unfortunately, our closest neighbour had taken it upon himself to be our enemy. It took a long time for us to work out why. The obvious conclusion was that he hated the English, but there was more to it than that. It was all a question of territory – and, more to the point, of terraces. We had one, he did not. Through some quirk of Napoleonic law we were co-proprietors of what we had dubbed "the studio". We owned the top two thirds, while he had possession of the ground floor, or *cave*. And, for some reason lost in the mists of time, the terrace between the two buildings had fallen to our lot.

For many years this bizarre division of property mattered not at all. Our co-proprietor was the *Notaire*; he only used the building which adjoined the divided property and rarely appeared at his kitchen window, which overlooked our terrace. As far as we knew, the *cave* was disused.

Then the *Notaire* moved out and Loony Tunes, as we came to know him (but only when we were being polite) moved in. The first tiny cloud on the horizon came in the shape of a belligerent little man with a big moustache covering what Himself refers to as an anus mouth.

One day he shouldered his way up to my husband in the street and, standing on tiptoe, eyed him accusingly in the top shirt button. I'm sure the speech he made – and it was a long one – was eloquent. Unfortunately, I was not there to hear it and it was wasted on Patrick who in those days spoke no French and understood less.

Luckily a friend who was staying with us at the time managed to deduce that there was some kind of problem connected with our joint ownership of the neighbouring property. He explained that Madame, who spoke French, would soon be arriving and would be happy to sort out any problem.

Of course Loony Tunes did not stoop to paying a neighbourly call once he knew I was back in France. Instead I was rudely summoned one day from his kitchen window with the French equivalent of 'Oy! You!'

The problem turned out to be that, whenever it rained, water was getting into his *cave* from an opening which gave onto our back stairs. Not a difficult one to solve, one would have thought. Simply put in a proper window, *et voila*!

Ever ready to be the good neighbour, I invited him warmly to make use of our terrace if he needed outside access to the opening. We would have been only too ready to exchange pleasantries. No doubt a beer or a *pastis* would have been offered. Tools, if needed, would have been lent. We would have made another friend in the village.

It was not to be. Somehow, the simple remedy to the problem just didn't figure on Loony Tunes' agenda. And so began the Great War of Loony Tunes' Cellar.

What followed was a five-year reign of terror. Well, to be accurate, a five-year reign of petty annoyances, much hilarity and one nasty incident. Loony Tunes' preferred method of intimidation was to stand at his window and grin at us. Our response was to grin back, which for some reason he didn't seem to appreciate.

Then, boldly seizing the initiative, he cut our telephone wires. Not once but three times in succession. Not a smart move, that. The wires, which crossed his wall (by express permission of the previous incumbent) were cut in a place only he could reach. The PTT (telephone company), thrice-summoned, were not amused. They made a formal complaint to the police.

Another time he turned up on the doorstep muttering imprecations. The heavy accent, the heavy moustache and the heavy consumption of *vin rosé* – without which he was meek as a lamb – conspired to make these inaudible. His temper was not improved when this sortie was met with gales of laughter.

Things only got worse when we got to work on the studio - the two-room apartment directly above his *cave*. Disused for many years, it was a haunt of spiders and a handy place to store the garden chairs over the winter. But two extra rooms are hard to resist, and eventually we turned this space into a delightful summer kitchen/dining room, with a guest suite above. Loony Tunes was not impressed.

The summonses started to arrive.

Number one manifested itself in a letter from the departmental *préfecture*. It had come to their notice, said they, that we had constructed a terrace without planning permission. Our village was a historic one, listed with *Les Architectes des Bâtiments de France*, no less, and getting planning permission for anything as radical as a terrace was nigh-on impossible. As for going ahead without the required piece of paper, well, they didn't actually say so but they gave us the impression that they were dusting off the guillotine.

Pardon us, we said, but you have been misinformed. The terrace has been there since time immemorial. Or at least since before we bought the house. Our estate agent – name and address supplied – would be happy to confirm this. Come and see for yourselves, we suggested. Which they did: they came, and they saw. Then the man from the *préfecture* accepted a beer. We knew we had won that round.

Summons number two was a stern admonishment from Loony Tunes' insurers. His goods, in the *cave*, had been damaged by rain. Naturally we were responsible for this catastrophe. (It sounded a lot more impressive in French: '*à la suite de sinistre dégât des eaux ayant atteint le 3 juin 1996 les biens situés etc, votre responsabilité peut être engagée.*')

Not at all, we said. We have repeatedly offered M. *Untel* access to our terrace for the purpose of putting in a window to prevent just such an occurrence. We were not, we pointed out reasonably, responsible either for the rain or for the state of our neighbour's property.

There was a general convocation of insurers who, having inspected the offending site, came to a unanimous verdict: put in a window.

Loony Tunes was not amused. Thwarted, he took to pursuing us down the street bellowing 'You shall pay, and even Queen Elizabeth will know about it! We're not in England now!' I'm afraid there were tears. Indeed, Himself laughed so hard that I feared for his trousers. Loony Tunes didn't seem to see the joke.

For a long time our lunatic neighbour was nothing more than a source of amusing dinner party stories. Everyone has their neighbour-from-hell, and ours was up there with the best of 'em.

Until the day came when events took a sinister turn.

One New Year's Day our English neighbour, an inoffensive little old lady of seventy-something, myopically greeted Loony Tunes and wished him *Bonne Année*. She had mistaken him for someone she knew, and was unprepared for his response.

Fuelled by New Year cheer, Loony Tunes pounced. Pushing her aside he grabbed her spectacles from her nose, twisted them, threw them to the ground and stamped on them. Why? Just because she was English? Or because – perish the thought – he and the *vin rosé* mistook her for me? Luckily she was not hurt, though her glasses were broken, but naturally she was very shocked.

When she came to tell us what had happened I immediately rang the local police station. Of course, our gallant gendarmes positively sprang into action. 'Have you got a medical certificate?' said the bored voice on the end of the phone.

110

Let us pause for a moment to contemplate the noble French police force. No, on second thoughts, let's not. Suffice it to say, despite our accompanying the affronted Englishwoman to the police station, no action was ever taken.

Loony Tunes didn't have it all his own way, though: we did have one small and inadvertent revenge. One evening we were having a barbecue on the terrace. Someone dropped a chicken leg. It bounced. It rolled. And then we watched in horror as it shot unerringly into the opening in LT's wall and down into the black depths of his *cave*...

By this time we had engaged a lawyer, the tiny but fierce Maître B. And it wasn't long before our Pocket Rocket, as we called him, had gotten the measure of Loony Tunes. So when we told him the terrible tale of the chicken leg, he wept tears of glee. When we told him that we had actually penned an apologetic note and put it through Loony Tunes' door, he positively howled. After that, we were by a long shot Maître B's favourite clients.

We consulted Maître B regarding the third summons we received from Loony Tunes. This time our friendly neighbour had taken his complaint to the courts. An Expert would be summoned to view the iniquities we had inflicted on his property and his goods. On the day, Himself was not around for some reason, and was rather worried for my safety. Never fear, I reassured him, I'll have both Maître B and Jean-Jacques, the estate agent, to back me up. Two pocket rockets.

At 3 o'clock we were all assembled: Loony Tunes and his wife, Loony Tunes' *avocat*, my *avocat* and estate agent - plus, of course, The Expert.

First of all, they proposed to view the damage to our neighbour's property. 'I'm not having HER in MY house,' blustered Loony Tunes, well primed with *rosé*. So off they trooped to inspect the site, leaving me alone and palely loitering in my kitchen. Suddenly an enormous crash startled the air, followed by furious banging. It seemed to be coming from our terrace stairs. I shot out of the back door and across the terrace, shrieking like a banshee. 'What are you doing?' I yelled. 'Stop it at once or I'll call the police.' An empty threat, as those assembled knew all too well. However, the banging stopped.

Three minutes later they were all on the front steps of our house. An actor's blood runs through my veins and I can summon it at need. This day I decided to play Meek and Intimidated. I shrank back. I positively cowered. 'I don't want HIM in MY house' I echoed, but it was a whimper, not a sneer.

Loony Tunes was left outside, while the rest of the troop filed up the stairs, through the house and across the terrace to inspect the site from the outside. As Maître B passed me, he shot me a very sharp look. There was the ghost of a wink. We understood each other: Loony Tunes had effectively cooked his own goose.

It wasn't until much later that I found out what had happened. Showing the Expert the locale of his grievance, Loony Tunes had become so incensed that he totally lost it. He had started attacking his own wall with a sledgehammer, screaming obscenities the while. And his *avocat*, my *avocat*, the estate agent and the Expert looked on...

The Expert's verdict was swift and to the point: put in a window, he suggested.

Loony Tunes was quiet for a long time after that. No more grinning from windows, no street pursuits, no violence against little old ladies. Then one late summer evening I was doing a spot of gardening on the terrace. As I was watering the yucca I heard his window open. Oh, terror. Was he about to grin at me?

But no. There was a muffled harrumphing noise and then, unmistakeably, a voice pronounced my name. I looked up in astonishment, but politeness is engrained. '*Bonsoir*,' I said mildly. 'Not in the cellar, please' he said, indicating the hose. A joke? He had made a joke? I was gobsmacked.

And did I give him the finger and a well-deserved mouthful of abuse? Did I even grin at him? Not at all. We English know how to be gracious in victory. '*Bien sûr, Monsieur*,' I said demurely.

And thus it was that peace broke out on the terraces of our little village.

Gulliver Travels

It was a July day in our second or third summer as *Morbignanais*. It was hot. Nothing stirred. The village children had stopped yelling. The good ol' boys had left their bench under the plane tree in the square and gone home for their midday *pain et vin*. Lizards were curled up in the cracks in our dry-stone wall, dreaming no doubt of juicy grapes.

We had finished our lunch and the water in our glasses was growing tepid; the bubbles flat and the ice a distant memory. The afternoon stretched before us. Thoughts of siestas in cool shuttered rooms were beginning to coax us from our lethargy.

Then, in quick succession, there was a whirr, a shout of alarm from Himself, a scrabble, a squeak, a slither and a thump. A small, angry bundle of fluff and feathers sat on the table and glared at us. Gulliver had arrived.

Of course, we didn't know at the time that it was Gulliver. We didn't in fact know what he was, although we realised his parents probably belonged to the summer-visitor group. Our terrace was loomed over by the crumbling tower of the thirteenth-century church. Every summer hundreds of birds would gather and nest there, and every evening they would emerge for the feeding frenzy...

We'd often debated their species: swifts, swallows, house martins? What use bird books and details of markings when all we saw of them were fast-moving silhouettes against a dazzling or darkening sky?

Then we found the answer. Swifts, according to the bird book, have "vigorous, dashing flight, wheeling, winnowing and gliding; excited parties chase each other squealing around the houses in small towns and villages". Yes! That was just how our summer birds behaved.

The birds would cease flight only to nest and lay their eggs. Year after year we would see their offspring make their first tentative forays into the wider world, to the anxious encouragement of their parents. During our summers in France we had seen many baby casualties who had launched themselves from high roosts on unsteady wings and optimism. Sadly many came to grief, and not all survived the adventure.

Now here was Gulliver. We quickly named him so, because of his heroic travels and because, well, if he was a swift, the name was perfectly appropriate. Mind you, he didn't look remotely like what the bird book said a swift should look like: 'an all-black bird with graceful swept-back wings and a forked tail'. His tail was stubby and he had a fawn band on his back and a fawn underbelly. But he was a baby, so perhaps he would grow into the bird-book image.

The immediate problem was what to do with him. I found a small cardboard box and crumpled some paper towel into it, then scooped him up and put him in. He didn't seem too grateful for the rescue. In fact, he tried to peck me. We settled him in the shade on the wide window sill and left him to recover from the shock of his crash. At seven o'clock I went to look at him.

Astonishingly, he was still alive. I let him out of the box, hoping that he would find his wings, but he did no such thing. He just squatted on the window sill, looking daggers at me. I had no idea what to feed a baby bird, so I tried him with a crumb of sandwich, with a bit of lettuce still clinging to it. It disappeared in no time, so I fed him some more. Now there was the question of water. Do birds drink? I put a saucer of water beside him. He surveyed it balefully for a moment, and then turned his back. I turned him around and dunked his beak. He struggled, he spluttered, he tried again to peck me – but some of the water must have gone in.

We had Gulliver for over a week. We kept him in his cardboard box in the shade all day, and in the evenings encouraged him to explore and try out his wings. We taught him to drink water. We continued to feed him on table scraps. The one time I managed to catch an insect he turned up his beak at it.

At first he showed no interest in flying. When his aunts and brothers and cousins swooped overhead in their ceaseless quest for insects, he would look up at them scornfully, as if to say, 'You have to *work* for a living?' Then one day he went missing. I hunted frantically, and finally found him at the foot of the cellar stairs. He must have flown down, because as far as I could see he was uninjured. Flying back, however, seemed to be beyond him.

'Well, what are you going to do about it?' was the clear challenge in his stare. I returned him to the patio. It was a turning point, though. No more heroic dives down the cellar steps, but every evening he would creep to the edge of the window sill and try out his wings, inevitably crash-landing in a heap of indignant feathers. Every evening he fluttered a little further.

One afternoon I was on the terrace, sunbathing. Suddenly Gulliver began to climb up the house wall.

116

Sensing something was afoot, I called urgently to my husband, 'You'd better get out here fast. I think Baby is leaving home.' Gulliver climbed on up steadily until he reached the guttering on the roof. Then he turned and looked at us. I could almost hear him say, 'Watch me! Mum! Dad! Watch me!'

He launched himself into space. We held our breath. He tumbled through the air and we tensed for a rescue mission. He began to climb, airborne this time. As he rounded the church another bird swooped down and flew beside him. We felt proud and tearful – we had reared our first chick.

Finding Adolf

'Impossible. Can't be done.' P'tit Gui glanced round the little room and shrugged his shoulders. Without a word, my husband handed him the folded sheet of graph paper. There was a long silence while Gui studied the paper, glancing up once or twice. He scribbled a calculation, he took out his tape measure, he dug under his baseball cap to scratch his ear with his pencil. 'But this is to scale,' he said. Himself shrugged modestly. Another pause ensued, then Gui squared his shoulders. '*Alors…*'

In the headlong rush of love that had followed our first sight of the Morbignan house, we hadn't paid much attention to the second guest room. To reach the main bedroom you turned right off the staircase, through a short tunnel, and took three steps across this small dusty room. Not exactly onerous.

After all, our main guest room was downstairs, next to the shower room and loo. Our guests often said how handy this was in the middle of the night, but remarked that its hideous ice-cream décor of raspberry, blackcurrant and vanilla was not conducive to calm when you woke up the morning after an evening of revels.

More to the point, the loo was downstairs and the master bedroom was up – not always that convenient to the master and mistress of the house. After a couple of years of living with midnight trudges down the stairs, we came up with a Plan. The little second bedroom would make an ideal *en suite*. Of course, it would be preferable if we could avoid a repetition of that Paris hotel where the only access to the bedroom was through the bathroom.

Now Patrick is good with plans. While I wave a vague hand in the direction of a wall and announce I want a doorway there, he measures and calculates. He's also remarkably good at fitting quarts into pint pots. When we bought our London flat, the 4 x 2.5m kitchen was so tiny that the previous incumbents had put the fridge in the corridor. By the time Himself finished with it he had installed not only the fridge but a washing machine, cooker and dishwasher too.

He assembled his tools: squared paper, pencil, ruler, tape measure, coffee. After a few hours he emerged, looking pleased. There on the paper was the most delightful bijou bathroom. It had a separate loo, with its own door. It had a huge shower cabinet and a three-quarter length bath. There was space for a princely sink unit. And, best of all, there was a short corridor along one side so we could go to and from the bedroom without disturbing anyone's ablutions.

Once P'tit Gui had got over the shock of seeing proper plans drawn up by a client – and an English client to boot – he and his merry men got to work. Not immediately, no – that is not the Midi way – but eventually the workforce arrived.

The working day would go something like this:

The alarm clock chirrups. This is a polite prelude to clearing its throat and squawking malevolently in my ear. Quarter to eight. Oh my god – Henri! He's coming this morning to build a wall and he'll expect coffee at 8 sharp.

Henri, the plasterer and bricklayer, is sixty-something and tiny – a handsome, bawdy bantam-cock of a man. On the dot of eight he arrives. '*Où est le chef?*' he demands. Himself is still asleep. Himself can sleep for Europe, especially in the mornings when there is *café* to be prepared against the onslaught of *les ouvriers*.

'*Il fait dodo*,' I explain apologetically. Henri laughs with a wink: he is convinced that we spend our nights in wild sexual excess and our mornings sleeping it off. Henri himself has no shortage of girlfriends. There are those he takes dancing and those, we gather, he takes to bed.

At that moment Patrick staggers in. '*Bonjour, chef*' booms Henri with a bone-crushing handshake. Himself winces and mutters *bonjour*.

The coffee drunk, the civilities done with, Henri gets ready for work. This involves donning his working gear – an old and battered pair of carpet slippers and an equally battered white linen hat shaped like a flower pot. His approach to dress and hygiene while at work is idiosyncratic, to say the least. Dressed to go out, he is resplendent.

I (and no doubt he) will never forget the sultry summer day when, near clocking-off time, I innocently mounted the stairs to offer a glass of something cool. Henri was on the landing – stark naked and washing himself in a bucket of water. For maybe five seconds we looked at each other with a wild surmise, then I fled. We have never, ever referred to the incident since.

Henri has a voice that can shatter glass at 25 metres and is given to spectacular tantrums. As we peacefully sip the remains of our breakfast coffee we'll hear the approaching storm. First a prolonged muttering, as of distant thunder. A crash: Henri has thrown whatever implement he is using to the ground. An explosion of 'Merde, alors!' followed by more distant thunder. Stamping that shivers the timbers of the house. More

muttering. Silence. Then: 'La-di-dum, la-la-LAAA' –
Henri at peace has a singing voice that makes up in volume
for what it lacks in tunefulness. The storm has passed
overhead and all is calm once more.

When P'tit Gui came to survey progress on the
bathroom, he and Henri (and whoever else happened to be
around) would indulge in a spot of what we came to call
synchronised shouting. No-one listened to anyone else.
The walls of our house flexed and trembled and Maman,
our robust ghost, clapped her hands over her ears and
muttered darkly. Was this, we would wonder, a terminal
bust-up? Were insults being hurled? Was P'tit Gui's
ancestry being impugned? Not at all: it was simply an
amicable discussion of the work in hand.

Slowly the bathroom took shape. After the bangs
and crashes, the shouting and the imprecations, the meals
gritty with plaster dust, came the excitement: choosing the
paint, the mirror, the marble sink top. And oh, the fun of

decorating! It was, I said firmly putting down my size four, to be blue, white and silver. And so we scoured the *bricos* for the exact shade of paint, we searched Komako and Gifi and Conforama for dark blue soap dishes and silver candle holders. A kind friend sewed navy and white striped curtains, another donated a set of matching bath towels, yet another came up with half a dozen decorative blue and white ceramic knobs for the cupboard doors.

At last it was ready. Barely containing our excitement, we invited P'tit Gui in to have a look. We flung open the little door and waited for his reaction. He sniffed at the blue-painted floorboards, curled a lip at the blue and white striped ceiling. He ran his finger over the glossy marble wash stand, twiddled the taps, grinned at himself in the film star mirror (complete with a frame of light bulbs), averted his eye from the illicit electric socket installed by Himself.

He gazed into the bath, scorned the heated towel rail, swung the door of the shower, peered round the corner into the separate loo, nodding approvingly at the matching blue-painted cabinet that just fitted snugly above the toilet – a present from our Ipswich friends. There was a long silence. Then P'tit Gui bestowed the highest compliment a *maçon* can pay his client. Solemnly, he shook Patrick's hand. '*Pas mal, chef,*' he said, '*Pas mal.*'

Flushed with triumph, we planned further building projects. We converted the 'studio' – the two upper rooms of the building across the terrace - into guest quarters. The lower floor became a kitchen/diner, ideal for summer lunches, and even dinners, when it was just too hot to sit out on the terrace. We left the old granary staircase in place, leading to a double guest bedroom with *en suite*.

Now we had our splendid new guest quarters, the ice cream spare room was the next matter on the agenda.

It would, we thought, make a good dining room. A bit of sprucing up, I thought, a lick of white paint and job done. I should have known better.

On one of those sultry Midi afternoons when the grey sky sprawls wetly on the rooftops and the temperature and humidity climb off the scale, Himself wandered into our projected dining room. 'I wonder,' he mused, 'what is under that plaster.' I winced. I begged and pleaded, but all to no avail: off he went to fetch his hammer and a cold chisel. After a few experimental taps he took a mighty swing, and a large chunk of plaster crashed to the floor. I was almost afraid to look. Were my worst fears realised? Not a bit of it: under the plaster was a wall of rough stones. Now, exposed stone walls were *über* fashionable in those days, and it seemed we had one ready-made.

My husband set to with a will, and an hour or two later the whole wall was exposed, at which point I gently suggested that perhaps he might put away his hammer and chisel. One feature wall would be quite enough.

He looked at me boot-faced. His lower lip came out. Oh dear, I thought, we were in for a confrontation of monumental proportions. Then his gaze travelled upwards. 'I wonder,' he mused, 'what's underneath that plaster.'

The ceiling had massive square-section plaster struts running across it which, I was convinced, concealed nothing more picturesque than rigid steel joists. However, I'd learned my lesson so I kept quiet as Himself climbed on a chair, chisel in hand. What was underneath that plaster, it turned out, were the original wooden beams, gnarled and blackened and iron-hard.

This was no job for an enthusiastic amateur, so we called in our friend Boris, who was a wizard with all things wood. It took him a week of chipping and cursing, but

123

eventually the beams were liberated from their plaster coffins; then all we had to do was treat and stain the beams and paint the plaster between them white. It was a long, slow, tedious job but at the end of it our dining room ceiling was a thing of wonder.

The room was beginning to take shape nicely, but there was still the small matter of three raspberry pink walls, an industrial grey windowsill and wallpaper blinding with pink and purple and cream and lilac flowers.

Careful chipping and the lightest of sanding took the grey paint off the window sill to reveal decorative tiling. We were discovering treasure after treasure (what on earth were the previous owners thinking, painting over those lovely tiles?) but the room had one more surprise in store for us.

Painting the raspberry walls only took a matter of three or four coats of brilliant white paint: we calculated that it would fade down soon enough to an acceptable cream. The remaining wall, the largest, was papered. We could have painted that too. We should have painted that too. Instead, in a rush of let's-do-it-properly-for-once, Himself decided to strip the paper off.

Perhaps it wasn't the best idea to do this in the middle of the summer. Even with its thick walls and tiny window the little room was stifling to begin with. When Himself got to work with what he liked to call his Hot Stripper, hired from the Kiloutou in St Rémy, it was unbearable. I used the oldest trick in the world for getting out of unwanted jobs: 'Can I help?' I offered. I was immediately assigned the task of providing refreshing drinks from our comparatively cool and airy kitchen. It never fails.

Three weary days later and the horticultural wallpaper lay in bright curls and tatters on the tiled floor, the plaster beneath it smooth enough, after some judicious sanding, for its coat of white. Reaching for the paintbrush, Himself stopped in his tracks. In the darkest corner was a scrawl of black, a graffito. There was a heart. There was an arrow through it. And on either side of the heart were the initials AH and EB.

We gave this some thought. We knew the previous owners of the house: neither of their names could be abbreviated to AH or EB. We enquired among our older friends in the community: no, nobody knew of a romance between anybody with those initials. Then some bright spark wondered aloud if it was possible, if it was remotely possible…

We knew the Germans had occupied the south of France. We knew the furthest reaches of their stamping ground included the Languedoc. Could the Führer have slipped away to a rural tryst with his beloved Eva?

Well, it's the sort of thing you want to believe, isn't it? So for a day and a half of wild excitement we pretended to think that our house had once sheltered the most evil man of the 20th century. It was Patrick who eventually burst the bubble. Peering closely at the inscription he concluded: 'I don't think they had permanent markers in the 1940s.'

* * * * *

We didn't paint over that patch. We covered the whole wall in book cases instead; I like to think that someone, in the far future, will dismantle the book cases, see the inscription and wonder if it was possible, if it was remotely possible…

Life in the Slow Lane

From: patricia@thestonehouse.fr
Sent   july 2 2004
To: jennie.el@cheylesmore.com
Subject: keeping busy

Hello again

Sorry, I know I promised you a longer email asap, but life round here has been rather frantic of late. Yeah, right, I hear you say! Well let me tell you, Miss London-is-the-only-place-to-live, that life down here is just as busy, just as buzzy and just as much fun as it was in the Smoke. More, so, in fact, because in a small village our friends are two streets away rather than half way across the city. So no, we are not stagnating down here, far from it.

   Mind you, it's taken a bit of getting used to. You know me, I'm an orderly sort of person, on the whole. I make plans. I write lists. Sometimes I stick to the plans. Once in a while I achieve the things on the lists – or at least some of them. I put it down to being raised in northern climes. Life was real, life was earnest when I was growing up. Not for us the lazy, hazy, *laissez-faire* temperament that took life as it came and went with the flow. *Mañana* was definitely not our thing. We never dropped in on people unannounced, and we expected fair warning if someone planned to visit us.

So just because Patrick and I have decided to up-sticks for the wilds of rural southern France, it didn't mean that I was going to fall victim to those decadent southern ways – or so I thought.

Take yesterday for example. We knew Ludo (he's the neighbour I told you about, whose wife ran off with the baker) was coming round at 8 sharp to work with Himself on some building project he has in hand. So at 7:45 there I was in the kitchen – which of course was clean and tidy - making coffee.

Well, all right, it wasn't exactly 7:45. We did oversleep, but that was only because Hanneke and Heidi called round unexpectedly last night and we drank a glass or two of wine. And yes, if you insist, there were a couple of glasses and a few plates in the sink, and a bowl which had contained olives. But the intentions were good.

What actually happened was this. At 8:10 there was a loud banging on the front door. Himself opened a bleary eye and said 'Oh, dear, I think that's Ludo.' He stumbled downstairs and a mere three minutes (oh, all right, ten) later I followed to make apologies and coffee.

That's when things got sternly back on track. Patrick and Ludo drank their coffee and set about their first task of the day: clearing up the workshop. This was to be followed by a run up to the local tip. Meanwhile I finished the washing up and was working on my shopping list – eggs, kitchen paper, more red wine (where *does* Hanneke put it?) – when Mighty Mouse turned up. I can't wait for you to meet Mighty Mouse. She's my next-door neighbour – insofar as we have a next door, I told you about the geography of the village. She's absolutely tiny but she has a very determined personality, and a voice to match.

She wanted to know if we had any wood treatment products in our garage. A simple '*Non*' would have sufficed, but we don't do things like that round here. It would be considered rude. So instead we chatted for a half-hour or so about my garden (potted) and her garden, her husband and mine, the chances of the Tramontane (the local wind – fierce!) dying down and the temperature going up. Normal civilities.

Eventually she left in search of wood stain and more conversation and I walked with a purposeful air to the hall cupboard to get my jacket. I checked the inventory: shopping list, car keys, carrier bags... and the gate squeaked.

I think I've probably told you about our front gate, it's our early warning system. Over the years countless well-meaning builders and even a few friends have offered to apply a drop of oil, but we are having none of it. It takes so long to get that front gate open, and the process is so noisy, that we have ample time to a) get the kettle on / the wine uncorked or b) hide and pretend to be out. Usually a combination of sociability and nosiness makes us tend towards the former.

So there I was, with stern purpose writ on my brow, when Chérie opened the gate. She had come in search of Ludo, who's her partner. Of course I had to offer her a cup of coffee, it was only common courtesy. And that was when Alice, my next-door neighbour on the other side, appeared. Alice is English, seventy-something, nosy as a cat and deaf as a post, but she can still hear the kettle being put on anywhere within a half-mile radius. 'Oh, were you making tea?' she asked, all innocence. I wasn't, but I did.

By this time it was getting on for *midi,* and with wifely intuition I suspected that Patrick and Ludo had gone off to the café to celebrate their morning's efforts. Sure enough, the phone rang: it was Himself to say they were, surprise surprise, at the café. Why didn't we pop over and join them, he said.

This seemed like a good idea, but just as we were about to leave M. Planète walked in to show us he was alive. He got himself knocked down two days ago by Gui (our local tearaway — all of twelve years old) on his *mobilette*, and was now making a stately progress round the village to assure his friends and neighbours of his recovery. Once again the kettle went on.

Then just as it looked as if Alice and M. Planète were on their way, and we could finally set off for the café, my friend Bubbles rang up for a girly gossip… Yes, really: Bubbles! How awful is that? The first time I met her we were both in the ladies' loo at the Café de l'Ane in St Rémy. She knew us by sight – well, all the ex-pats know each other down here – and she came over to introduce herself. 'Hello,' she said, 'my name is Bubbles.' I tell you, I very nearly said 'Oh, you poor thing' but I managed to turn it into 'Oh, yes, you live in that big house on the way to St Azeph, don't you?'

Actually she's very nice, and so is her husband: tall, distinguished-looking and frightfully well-spoken! So there we were, chatting away – Chérie gave up and went over to the café and I finally joined them all about half an hour later for a pre-lunch drink. It was a gorgeous day (so there!), so we sprawled on the café terrace in the sunshine telling each other how hard we were going to work during the afternoon and how much we were going to accomplish.

A glass or two later, as we headed back for a bite of lunch before getting down to it in earnest, we bumped into Sainte-Thérèse. Sainte-Thérèse is married to M. Planète, and with four children and countless animals to look after she has a lot to put up with, which she does with a good deal of dry humour. 'Oh, you all looked so relaxed sitting outside the café, I was just about to come and join you,' she said wistfully.

Thinking she was on her own, I invited her to come and join us for a quick lunch. 'Lovely,' she said, 'I'll just go and get the family…' Ten minutes later she turns up in my kitchen with two children and M. Planète in tow! She brought all sorts of provisions – cheese and *charcuterie*, bread and wine, as well as crisps and crabsticks (yuk!) for the children – and so we pooled our resources like loaves and fishes and settled down to an impromptu picnic on our microscopic front terrace. All thoughts of a working afternoon disappeared.

By half past four the wine was flowing and the jokes were getting sillier. Ever tried translating a pun from French to English, or vice versa? Take my word for it, it ain't easy. By six o'clock we were playing bilingual charades with the children. At seven Thérèse departed to pick up another child from his friend's house. At eight M. Planète and daughters finally left. At eight ten the Planète daughters reappeared: '*Maman* has gone off with the key and we can't get into the house…' At eight fifteen, luckily, Thérèse returned, with child and key, to assemble her brood.

They all finally left at about eight thirty, by which time all we could do was collapse in exhaustion over yet another glass of wine. But, we told each other, we'll really get down to some work tomorrow. That's today, by the way, so I'd better bring this email to a close before I get derailed again.

So if you really want to know how we pass our time, now we are semi-retired and have no jobs to go to: no, we don't get bored and no, time doesn't hang heavy on our hands. We've got plenty to do, I promise you. It's finding the time to do it that's the problem!

Lots of love to you and Peter

P xxx

Town hall blues

Although our new guest quarters and *en-suite* bathroom
were a triumph, they did throw up a few problems. When
we had acquired the house in Morbignan, it had one loo,
one shower, one hand basin and a couple of sinks. And one
valiant little water heater on the wall above the kitchen
sink served them all.

By the time the latest round of building works was
completed we had, we discovered, three loos, three hand
basins, two showers, a bath, two kitchen sinks and a
laundry room in the *cave* with washing machine and
industrial-sized sink. One little water heater just couldn't
cut it.

The bath took three quarters of an hour to fill and
came out lukewarm because the hot water ran out half way
through the filling. Showers were apt to be interrupted by
shrieks as the warm spray from the nozzle turned frigid
without warning.

When we had guests we had to warn them that they
should let us know if they were planning a shower: if the
kitchen tap went on at the same time, the result was apt to
be unpleasant.

There was no help for it: it was time to find a
bigger *chauffe-eau*. First of all we had to locate the
plumber. Like P'tit Gui the builder, M. Dujardin was
competent, reliable (by Midi standards) and reasonably
affordable – all of which meant that he was just as in-
demand, and just as hard to run to earth, as the elusive
maçon.

I put out the word – through P'tit Gui, through Josiane, through my network of village spies, as well as by the more mundane method of leaving ever more frantic messages on his answering machine – and came the day M. Dujardin turned up on the doorstep. 'I've been meaning to come and see you,' he said without preamble. 'I think you are going to need a bigger *chauffe-eau.*' This was no surprise, really, as M Dujardin himself had installed the various appliances, but it did lead me to wonder why he hadn't said so at the time.

After much discussion, and after poring over the catalogue he had helpfully brought along, we selected a huge and fearsome beastie of many hundreds of litres of capacity. This, he suggested, could live down in the *cave.*

As I have mentioned, in the old village houses of rural France the *cave* is likely to be not the cellar but the ground floor, and so it was in our house. It had an old entrance, long blocked off, which in the past would have allowed the farmer to bring his beasts into their ground-floor stabling. Given that the walls of the house are several feet thick, this entrance is in fact a short tunnel. Perfect: we'll put the new water heater in there, we thought.

Town gas hadn't yet reached our village, and up till then we had been making do with small gas bottles which we could refill at the garage or supermarket. The fearsome beastie, of course, would consume a lot more gas than the small kitchen water heater so we decided we'd switch to the bigger bottles which you could have delivered. There was plenty of room to store these in the *cave*, we thought innocently.

M Dujardin duly started work, and then one day he stopped, gulped a bit and said 'oops' (or the French equivalent). This was not reassuring. One thing you do not want is a French plumber saying oops. It turned out we were not allowed to have the big bottles inside the house because they were butane (or was it propane?) and dangerous, as opposed to the little bottles which were propane (or butane?) and safe.

P'tit Gui, when consulted, was quite sanguine. 'No problem,' he cried. 'We'll unblock the old street entrance. Then we'll build a wall across the tunnel, half way down, and put the water heater on it. The bottles can stand behind it, on the other side of the wall, in a recess open to the street, which will be both safe and legal.'

The word 'legal' rang an awful bell. Naturally we needed to get permission to punch said hole in the street wall, and that meant dealing with the *Mairie*. At first we were confident: after all, according to P'tit Gui, he and the Mayor were practically blood brothers. We had obtained other permissions, surely a little thing like re-opening a previously existing doorway couldn't present too many problems?

We had reckoned without French bureaucracy.

Papers had to be submitted. First there was a long and complicated form to be filled in, enquiring into the minutiae of the property to be developed. Much head-scratching ensued. Was it, we wondered, a construction not creating floor space? Was the house perchance classified under legislation regarding historic monuments (it was)? And what was the *exact* nature of the work we wanted to do? Opening up a doorway was, it seemed, too simple a proposition.

To this form should be appended detailed plans of the proposed work, with sketches and dimensions; photos of the site to be developed and a copy of the land registry document (*cadastre*). Oh and by the way, they wanted it all in quintuplicate.

Well, we did all that. And just as we were congratulating ourselves on a job well done, the secretary in the *Mairie* smiled at us sweetly and said 'That's fine. You should have an answer in three months.'

In the meantime the magnificent new *chauffe-eau* brooded on the wall of the *cave*. The little kitchen water heater chuffed and puffed and did its best. Baths still took three quarters of an hour to fill. The new shower would have been the ideal solution – it had its own water heater - except that the shower had no door on it. The plumber, who was going to order and fit the new door, had disappeared again.

We bore this stoically for a month, then tempers snapped. Enough was enough. I rang P'tit Gui and said publish and be damned – meaning let's go ahead with the opening and to hang with building permission. It was after all only a re-opening - you could clearly see where the door had been.

P'tit Gui thought he had better inform the town hall, just to be on the safe side. And, wonder of wonders, the mayor himself rang to say he was trying to contact *L'Architecte des Bâtiments de France*, no less, and could it wait a bit? I said yes, but we had to have the opening made before we left for a holiday in England. When would that be, he enquired. September 15 I lied – a matter of some three weeks away. Naturally permission didn't materialise within the time but, with lightning speed by French civil service standards, we got a letter on the 30th. No objection was being raised.

And so, a mere four and a half months after deciding we needed to install a new water heater, the new water heater was installed. The actual work took half a day.

* * * * *

It was an inspired moment. We were on our way back to England, still shell-shocked from our battles with the town hall. To pass the journey we often used to play word games, and 'collectives' was one of our favourites. It's a case of devising apt and quirky collective nouns for various professions: a pipe of plumbers, a spark of electricians and so forth. 'Now what would be the collective word for French civil servants?' pondered Himself.

'Easy,' I replied quick as a flash. 'A 'NON!' of French civil servants, of course.'

Fêtes worse than death

As anyone who has lived in a small village in France will agree, the French are a festive lot. Any excuse will do to fire up the barbecue, lay out the long tables under the trees in the *place*, dust off the village mascot – in our case a rather bedraggled cockerel – and send *'Allo 'Allo* into a frenzy of reminding us to reserve our places by Tuesday evening *at the very latest*. Naturally no-one bothers, and come the eve of the *fête* you'll see the queue of villagers outside the *Mairie* waiting to pick up their tickets. Everyone always gets in, of course.

Newcomers beware: there are strict rules to this kind of occasion. In the first place, festivities start at seven sharp, but it's best to be at your table by six if you want to bag the best seats. Secondly, food is plentiful, crockery and cutlery are not: you bring your own. On occasions you even have to bring your own chairs, too. The menu is fairly standard: undercooked *moules*, overcooked *brochettes*, bread and wine a-plenty. The trick is in the supplements.

The first time we went to a village 'do' we thought ourselves very clever to have brought some nibbles to accompany the apéros: olives and a tube of *Crousti 'Croc* (the French equivalent of Pringles). We were sure our table-mates would be delighted with our *largesse*. Until, that is, Josiane arrived, followed by an enormous cool box under which labored mightily her beleaguered husband Gérard. It was just like the scene in "The Wind in the Willows" where Rat tells Mole what's in the picnic basket. There was pâté, there was cheese, there were olives and

138

slices of *saucisson*. There were even pretty paper napkins. Josiane had come prepared.

All this, of course, is quintessentially French. But, some seventeen years after we bought the Morbignan house and two years into our full-time residency, the villagers discovered, to their amazement, that there were English living among them. And decided to do something about it.

The invitation that dropped though my letter box was a little different from the usual photocopied announcement. I opened the envelope and withdrew the crisply folded sheet of paper. The *Foyer Rural*, it said, would be delighted to entertain the English of the village to tea.

This was a first. Our village was by no means hostile to the ever-growing community of ex-pats, but generally a polite '*bonjour*' fitted the bill – they weren't exactly effusive, either. But here they were offering to entertain us on our own home ground, so to speak.

Came the day, and I have to admit to feeling ashamed. Only four English managed to drag themselves to the rooms of the *Foyer Rural*, where we stood around looking polite, bewildered and not a little embarrassed. Why no-one else made the effort I don't know. Perhaps they never got the invitation.

The locals did us proud. There were rock cakes and little pastries and even tea, as well as wine and pastis to stiffen the resolve of all and sundry. A lot of energetic smiling went on and some conversation too – and then our Oldest Inhabitant got out his clarinet. No *fête* or gathering in our village was complete without the oldest inhabitant and his clarinet. 'God Save the Queen', he played, to rousing applause, and 'La Marseillaise' to even the score.

Entente Cordiale was well and truly established.

Well, naturally, we had to reciprocate. My neighbour Penny was a superb pastrycook. We had a shady terrace and Patrick had a mean hand with the Pimms. We decided to throw caution to the winds and put on a full-scale English tea party. It was a risk, of course. Hospitable though they might be, our neighbours were cautious. Putting on a little tea party in the safety of the *Foyer Rural* was one thing. Venturing over the threshold of an English household for an arcane ritual such as this was quite a different matter.

We had no idea if anyone would come, but ever-hopeful we sent out the invitations. Naturally, no-one responded, but nonetheless on the appointed day we rolled up our sleeves and prepared the feast. Penny made scones and an iced Victoria sponge. I cut cucumber sandwiches and scoured Intermarché for biscuits and the finest jam – *Bonne Maman*, of course. There were a few late strawberries still to be had in the markets, and although clotted cream was beyond us I discovered well-chilled *crème épaisse* was almost as good. We borrowed a tea urn – from the *Foyer Rural* as it happened - and Himself unearthed a bottle of Pimms and got busy with the makings.

And they came. On the hottest day of the year, they came. Dozens of them. *Le Foyer Rural* was there of course. *La Mairie* was represented (though not the Mayor himself of course). The ladies from the stretching class and the ladies from the pottery class turned up *en masse*. Jean Paul from the café was there, along with his wife and three of his children. Others came, curious to see how these English live. They sipped tea and drank Pimms and did not find them wanting. They ate strawberries and cucumber sandwiches and came back for more. They loaded scones dubiously with cream and jam and discovered they liked them. They chattered and laughed and seemed to have a jolly good time. The English among us entertained graciously. And then the Oldest Inhabitant got out his clarinet…

But the greatest accolade was still to come. Later that evening, when tired but triumphant we sauntered into the bar for a well-earned drink, Jean-Paul greeted us rapturously. '*Attention tout le monde*,' he bellowed, '*voici les 'Morbignanglais.'*

The English, it seemed, had arrived.

Vive le Sport

It was the autumn of 1998 and I had gone into the post office to buy some stamps. The new issue had come out, covered in football images. 'Ah, yes,' I mused, 'now who was it who won the World Cup?'

'France,' said the little postmaster proudly.

'It wasn't Argentina, I don't think,' I continued as if I hadn't heard him.

'It was France,' insisted the postmaster, rather tetchily.

Of course,' I added, 'it might have been Germany. It's usually them.'

By now the little postmaster was almost apoplectic. 'France won the World Cup,' he said loudly. I grinned at him: we English do love to tease the French.

To be fair, they take it in good part. They know, and apart from a few mindless hooligans most sensible English people know, that we as a nation are rubbish at football.

Five years later it was the rugby world cup that was very much in the news in our little community. Now rugby is a horse of an entirely different colour. Not that I know anything at all about the sport – I don't – but there were plenty of people in the village to remind me that the English aren't all that bad with balls of the elliptical persuasion. The tournament progressed, the nations fell like ninepins until the semi-finals, when England faced France.

Because the game was taking place in Australia, it would be transmitted live during the morning. Jean-Paul, the café owner, announced he would open up early and install a large-screen television in the bar so we could all watch England being defeated by our gallant Gallic hosts. Of course it was Simon, the life and soul of all our village parties, who came up with the idea: why not do a full English breakfast for the spectators?

The village ladies rallied round, led by Simon's long-suffering wife Zizi. There would be eggs and bacon, of course. There would be sausages and toast. There would be black pudding and baked beans and mushrooms. There would of course be coffee and tea and orange juice, to which the more alcoholically-minded among us added Buck's Fizz.

Jean-Paul good-naturedly turned over the café kitchen to us, and on the morning of the match we got cooking. One by one the French drifted in to inspect, and turned their noses up at this outlandish ritual. Bacon? In the morning? Unheard-of. Champagne mixed with orange juice? Outrageous.

But as we doled out the brimming plates to the English spectators, and enticing smells began to creep out into the bar, there was a definite change of heart. Suddenly, and strictly in the name of *entente cordiale*, you understand, one by one the French members of the audience presented themselves sheepishly at the kitchen door. Was there, perhaps, just a little to spare?

As the last plate was satisfyingly wiped clean with the last morsel of toast, the game began. Roars of encouragement dwindled to a mutter as the English steadily made headway, Johnny Wilkinson the star of the day, of course. By half time the French among us were chanting the funeral march. And as the game closed, in torrential rain and mud, they generously congratulated us while we did our best not to smirk.

That, according to our friends and neighbours, was that. France was out of the tournament and the eventual outcome of the World Cup was of supreme indifference to them. Jean-Paul would not be importing a large screen for the final, though the old TV in the corner would no doubt be muttering away as usual. Still, there would be no convivial breakfast.

Simon, of course, was having none of it. *We* were still in the game, against Australia on their home ground, and the English community would support our brave lads to the end. Simon's house was across the road from the bar, so early drinkers were treated to the spectacle of a steady stream of England supporters making their way to *chez* Simon. This time there was no Full English – I suspect Zizi had put her foot down – but we all brought something – croissants, baguettes, pots of jam – and settled down to watch on Simon's rather more modest television.

The game see-sawed back and forth, racking up the tension. Every time England drew ahead, one of our number would rush across the road and make faces and rude gestures through the café window. Every time Australia scored, the French would reply in kind.

It went to extra time. The suspense was unbearable, and several of us fled to the kitchen so we wouldn't have to watch, but our ears were straining. Suddenly there was a collective intake of breath, followed by an almighty cheer from the *salon*. An English victory.

Solemnly we all trooped across the road, bowing and shrugging to imaginary roars of congratulation. The French in the bar were silent when we came in. To a man they rose to their feet; it was an uncertain moment. Then the applause began.

Our postmaster had retired by then, but we often saw him as we walked along the river, with his tubby little terrier who was one of Purdey's best friends. Two mornings after the rugby final we ran into him, and after the obligatory handshakes and remarks about the weather, he got down to the business in hand. '*Alors*,' he said, '*l'Australie a gagné?*' No, I informed him loftily, Australia had not won. He chortled, and I suppose he had the right: he had waited five years for his revenge.

Uba

I was just coming back from Intermarché, lugging the last carrier bag up our stone steps, when Mme Sériex came slowly up the street. I hadn't seen her for some months, and I hardly recognised her. She was limping, leaning heavily on a cane, and there was no sign of the little spaniel which usually trotted devotedly at her heels.

I thought back to the day we first met. Purdey and I were on our favourite walk, down by the river. It was late June and the Tarroux had dwindled to a trickle, barely lapping at the stepping stones that three months earlier had been completely submerged.

Unusually for a spaniel, Purdey is not a great fan of swimming. It has to be calm, and warm, before she will venture a dip. She was just cautiously contemplating a toe in the water when… WHAM! A small, solid, brown and white furry ball came hurtling out of nowhere and cannoned in to her. It was a Brittany puppy.

Purdey is normally good with puppies, but she was taken by surprise. She swatted the impudent youngster away - and over and over rolled the pup in a flurry of paws and fluff. Horrified, I was about to rush and rescue and soothe when I caught sight of the puppy's owner. A tall, dignified woman of some eighty summers, she was twinkling at me as she raised an admonitory finger. Wait!

Sure enough, the pup gathered herself up and, wriggling her entire bottom with delight, rushed back for more. This time, Purdey loftily granted an approving lick, and that was it. They were Best Friends Forever.

146

After that we often met Mme Sériex and the puppy, Uba. Purdey would spot them long before I did, and go hurtling down the path to fling herself with ecstatic wags and licks on the much smaller puppy. Uba never seemed to mind the rough treatment, which was Purdey's idea of love and affection, and Mme Sériex was one of those sensible dog owners who recognise play when they see it.

Today I had to disguise my shock. My upright, stately friend was suddenly an old woman. And where was Uba? I greeted Mme Sériex with cautious concern, asking about her health, not daring to mention the dog. I was careful to maintain the polite '*vous*' of a younger person to an older. And then she told me the tale.

'It's the arthritis, *mon chou*,' she explained. 'It has caught up with me at last: my days of walking by the river are over. 'Now I am as you see me, an old woman, tottering along. I had to give Uba to my son, it wasn't fair on the dog, I can't take her out any more. My beautiful Uba.' The fierce blue eyes softened and her voice caught. I helped her to the bench that stood by our wall, and as she sat Purdey trotted over to say hello, her absurd stump of a tail waggling furiously.

Mme Sériex put out her arms and Purdey, who never sits on anyone's knee but mine, jumped into her lap and pushed her head under the old lady's chin. Woman and dog cuddled close. I heard a noise like a sob and Purdey put out a pink tongue and licked at the salt that had fallen on to her muzzle.

A window on the world

Late in 2004 we decided to tackle The Spider Room. It was the last great building project: we now had our guest quarters, our master bedroom with *en-suite fantaisiste* and a stately dining room

Now the Spider Room. It had stood cobwebbed and unvisited off the top landing for as long as we had had the house. It had neither floor nor ceiling but – more crucially still – it had no window. In the days when our house was a village farmhouse, the Spider Room was probably a granary.

If we were to turn it into the superb second guest/sitting room we planned, we would have to get permission to cut a hole in the end wall of the house. Unfortunately said wall faced the church across a tiny *place* of no more than 20 metres. Even more unfortunately, our village was a very old one and a former *Maire* had thought it a jolly good wheeze to have the village itself declared of historic interest – that is, it came under the aegis of *L'Architecte des Bâtiments de France.*

This was a matter of some civic pride to the *Morbignanais*, but meant added difficulty for us. You couldn't lift a screwdriver – you couldn't so much as think about lifting a screwdriver - until that august body was consulted. And this, of course, could only happen through the intervention of the town hall. It was time to tackle the *Mairie* again:

We spoke to P'tit Gui, our kindly master builder. Was there any chance of getting that all-important *permis de construire*, we asked him. He sucked his teeth and thoughtfully poured himself another cup of coffee. Then his expression brightened. 'But of course,' he said, holding up crossed fingers. 'Me and the *Maire,* we're like *that.*'

It wasn't quite that easy, of course. We filled in umpteen forms. We made umpteen sketches. We went and saw the Maire and assured him we would of course build an absolutely traditional window. We waited three months and nobody said no. According to P'tit Gui, this meant yes, but we were more cautious. We waited two more months and – finally – written permission to build the window arrived. And that's when the fun began.

On Monday the workmen arrived – just as P'tit Gui had promised. Little Henri with his carpet slippers and cotton hat, his stories of culinary triumphs and gargantuan feasts, his girlfriends beyond number. He was accompanied, of course, by the obligatory Gormless Lad.

The obligatory coffee and cigarettes consumed, they got to work. There was a lot of banging, then silence. Reappearance of Henri, looking a tad worried. It seemed he thought the wall might fall down. That meant, in fact, the entire end of our house. Now we were looking worried. Henri bellowed for *un acrow* (adjustable prop), which was swiftly produced and put in place.

At this point we began to wonder if we would have steel girders propping up our ceiling and walls for the foreseeable future, but no: Henri whipped in a lintel and cemented it in place in no time flat.

On Tuesday night it rained, as only the Languedoc can. 'Did the wall hold up?' Henri asked cheerfully as he splodged up the steps. We hadn't dared look, but luckily it had. Work went ahead cautiously until, on Wednesday, a slot appeared in the wall. Actually, two slots appeared; the first one was misplaced. '*C'est pas mon boulot,*' Henri confided in us. This, he was telling us, was not his normal kind of work. It seemed he was only doing this as a favour to P'tit Gui. This was not reassuring. Did he in fact know what he was doing, we wondered. After all, he was the one with the sledgehammer knocking holes in our wall. Still, the lintel held good and the hole in the wall was beginning to look like a window.

It was Thursday when disaster struck. I was stumbling round the kitchen getting coffee under way when The Gormless Lad appeared on the doorstep. He had in tow a small, round, determined-looking man whom I had never seen before. TGL announced that he and Henri had got to go to another *chantier*. It seems P'tit Gui had promised they would lay a garage floor for another client. Small round man was the client, and he was not letting go. I knew how he felt, but… *tant pis*. I felt a Gallic shrug coming on.

Taking a deep breath, I let fly with an explosion of nuclear dimensions. I got on the phone to P'tit Gui. Madame answered: he had just left, of course. What, I demanded hotly, is his mobile number? Madame gave me the number with, I detected, a touch of glee. I phoned the mobile and P'tit Gui unwisely answered. At the first sound of my voice he started to bluster. It's only for today he protested – they'll be back with you tomorrow.

Then Henri arrived and I let fly at him for good measure. My French became more fluent than it had ever been before; I use words I didn't know I knew. I said things like '*pas sérieux*', which is about as bad an insult as you can hurl. Henri turned a little pale. I explained that I was not *engueul*-ing him, but I was sorely displeased with P'tit Gui and if things weren't sorted pronto the whole lot of them would be off the job.

Henri and The Gormless Lad went into a huddle. Plan C (subsection 4a) was rapidly brought into play. They would stay with me and work for the morning Henri conceded. Oh, and by the way, could he borrow an angle grinder?

At lunch time they broke for *paing et ving*, and long experience told me that we would not see them again that day. Would they please, I said, make sure someone came to block up the gaping hole in our end wall, so invitingly flanked by scaffolding? Needless to say they assured me with tears in their eyes that it would be done. Needless to say it wasn't. Patrick, who was busy working on another project, has to be hauled away to block up the window. He was not pleased, to put it mildly.

The climax came on Friday. It was the day Himself discovered, to the surprise of all, that he could speak French. Now Himself does not do languages. He does numbers. He does technical. He has a nice line in 'don't you bother your pretty little head about the practicalities.' But languages, no.

On Friday, all that changed. We had been at a *fête* for a friend's birthday. We had lunched not wisely but too well. Eventually tiredness and *angst* and general discontent caught up with Patrick and he went off to lie down in a darkened room. He returned an hour or so later looking not a little pleased with himself. 'I've just fired P'tit Gui,' he crowed. 'I rang him up and told him to get his (expletives deleted) workmen out of my house and off my *chanti*er.'

And that was all it took. P'tit Gui, who to this day still reminisces chortlingly about the time Himself gave him his marching orders, was unfazed. And when the time came to resume work once more, lo and behold all was peace and amity.

Of course, given that that Sunday was *Le Quatorze Juillet*, Monday was *férié* – a bank holiday. But when we returned on Monday from a trip to Carcassonne, where we had gone to view the celebrated fireworks, our *répondeur* was blinking furiously. Henri's voice informed us that P'tit Gui had phoned him (!) and told him to get his pert little bottom back to our house tomorrow and get on with the job. Himself's French was obviously better than we thought. Did we have lift-off? We dared to hope.

Come Tuesday at eight o'clock – no Henri, no Gormless Lad. Aha, thought we. But at two o'clock there they were, beavering away again.

On Wednesday there was steady progress all morning. Then – *catastrophe*! Where is the electrician? We need the electrician to move the socket so Henri can lay the floor. The floor had to be laid before the walls could be built, and the walls had to be built before the window frame could be fitted.

I had been chasing the electrician. P'tit Gui had been chasing the electrician. There had been no sign of the electrician for weeks. It looked like everything was going to grind to a halt again. Then Himself remembered that, in the days when he was a Gormless Lad himself, he trained as an electrician. Consternation on my part, but he seemed reasonably sure he could move the socket himself. But as he reached for the screwdriver there was a knock on the front door. It was the electrician. I swear they have antennae.

A day or two later I was once again in the kitchen preparing the essential *café*. There was a knock on the front door and when I opened it there on the doorstep stood a window frame. Peering closer, I could just make out the diminutive form of Thierry the carpenter propping up the frame. I greeted him like a long-lost brother: this was the final act of the window saga.

Thierry and frame disappeared upstairs where Henri was putting the final touches to the window. A lot of shouting ensued, but I was a veteran of many such encounters and remained unfazed. It was just builder and carpenter having an amicable discussion about the *pose* of the window frame.

Several hours later and – *voilà!* – there was a window where no window had been before.

The villagers had been following the fortnight's proceedings with increasing fascination. I had never had so many visitors who dropped in just casually to borrow a chair or offer a morsel of cheese from their own goats. It was time to reward such patience.

We decided to hold a small *apéro*. Naturally P'tit Gui and his workmen were the guests of honour. *M. le Maire* dropped in and the *Notaire* just happened to call. All our friends and neighbours were there. Even virtual strangers turned up: the *garagiste*, the *épicière*. Everyone crowded up the stairs to gawp at the splendid new window in the centuries-old wall. Then they all trooped outside to view it from the church square, murmuring approvingly at the Languedoc Cross we had tactfully (and tactically), had carved into the lintel stone.

Much still had to be done, of course: a proper floor was needed, and a proper ceiling. Then the room had to be decorated, and the outside of the house made good. We might be on our way to that *bijou* second guest room, complete with a view of the church, but in the meantime... it was time to call in P'tit Gui again.

Confessions of a vendange virgin

Every September and October, as the welcome cool weather finally returned to the Languedoc, we would witness the *vendange*, the grape picking. The fields were suddenly black with industriously bent backs and clanking machinery, the roads busy with pick-up trucks with their tottering loads of heady-smelling, faintly rotting grapes on their way to the *cave co-operative*.

Driving round the narrow lanes, with the westering sun in your eyes, you were apt to come face to face with tall, perilously swaying *vendange* machines heading in the other direction. Someone had to back up – it was usually the other driver, with a smile and a wave.

Every village had its *fête* to celebrate the harvest, usually with music and a barbecue, sometimes with fireworks. And these were true parties, not thinly disguised marketing events. One morning, after we had been royally entertained into the small hours of the night before, we thought it only polite to purchase a few bottles from the *cave* which had been our host. We'd sampled the wine, we had liked it, and it would have been rude not to. Or so we thought.

The *fête* itself had been in St Rémy, although the vineyards were some kilometres distant. We managed to locate the tiny village where the *cave* was, with the aid of a map and a friendly postman, and set off.

The path got narrower and narrower, steeper and stonier, until we were convinced we were on the wrong road. But no – just before we gave up in despair and turned

154

for home, we rounded a corner and there was the *cave*, standing foursquare, pink and slab-sided in the middle of a completely empty car park.

We ventured in. No-one was about. We loitered politely. We coughed Englishly. Eventually the *vigneron*'s wife appeared, wearing an apron and a puzzled expression. Could she help us? Well, yes, we explained, we'd come for the wine.

The wine? Her puzzled expression deepened. We might just have well have been enquiring for washing machines. Now we were confused: had we come to the wrong place? 'Is this Château X?' I asked her. Yes, indeed it was. And, I pursued, they did have a *fête* last night, where the local vintage flowed like tears at a wedding? 'Yes,' she replied, still looking bemused. 'Well, then we've come to buy some wine,' we explained.

Her expression cleared. Oh, no, she said. You can't *buy* the wine. It won't be ready until next September. What you had last night was just a sample of the *vigneron's* allotted stash.

So we were well accustomed to the spectacle and celebration of the *vendange*, but we had never actually participated, until the day that our friend and neighbour Antoine, who had a couple of tiny vineyards up in the hills, hinted that he could do with some grape pickers for a day or two's work – unpaid, of course, but well fed. Well, I thought, why not?

My husband was not impressed, but I pointed out reasonably that this was an experience we owed it to ourselves to experience. And anyway, I had volunteered, so that was that. As the day drew near and the September skies grew blacker and the rain fell in torrents day after day, it looked as if we would be off the hook. But the weather changed on the Monday, and on Tuesday Antoine was on the phone. 'It's time to pick the Merlot,' he announced. 'We've reached 13.3 degrees (of alcohol content) and now we have to get the crop in quickly – there's a bonus in it.' For him, I might add, not for us, but we had promised.

Wednesday dawned very black indeed, but that was because we were up and out of bed by 5:30 – an unprecedented hour for us. By the time the sun staggered blearily into the sky it was obvious we were in for a very fine day.

At eight on the dot we were up at the *mazet*, the little shepherd's hut in Antoine's vineyards. Or rather, we were in *sight* of the *mazet*. The already-assembled pickers could see us quite clearly from their vantage point on the heights, as we trundled up and down every track in the vicinity, assuring ourselves with diminishing conviction that we'd been here before, lots of times, and *surely* we knew the way?

Eventually, by a process of elimination, we found the right track, and roared up it to shrieks of derision. We needn't have worried, though: we were far from the last to arrive. The rest of the merry gang – we were nine in all – straggled in at intervals during the morning. After a day of picking, I understood why they – cannier by far than us innocents – had chosen to start later.

We were assigned our tasks and sent off with secateurs, two to a row to strip each side with maximum efficiency. Picture the scene: the grapes hang down in jewelled clusters, deep amethyst and succulent and ready to fall into your bucket at the merest snip. At least, that is the theory. The fact is that for every bunch that hangs down ripe for the picking, there is one that fiercely hugs the vine, the supporting wire and itself and defies you to detach it without a lengthy battle.

Working opposite your other half, I discovered, is the best option. There's an element of 'I'll reach that one for you' and 'Mind your fingers' and 'Let me carry that heavy bucket.' Working opposite the *patron* is the worst option. He picks tetchily and fast, leaving you far behind as you struggle with a recalcitrant bunch.

Then it was breakfast time. Sadly, there were no rustic benches, no long rough-hewn table spread with a checked cloth under the trees by smiling apple- cheeked old ladies. Instead it was a listing picnic table and several rather dubious folding chairs for seating.

But there were croissants and *fougasse*, cheese and *saucisson* and *pâté*, tea and coffee, chilled water and fruit juice – even beer and wine for those who could face it at 10 a.m. And the sun smiled down and the breeze cooled us and the view over the valley was glorious and we realised that *vendange* really is like every cliché you have ever read or seen in a movie.

I have to admit, though, that as the day wore on my mind was less on pastoral idyll than on screaming muscles. Bend, crouch, snip, kneel, bend, snip, lift – the person who invented the expression 'backbreaking' knew what he was talking about.

But every now and again the evocative shout of '*Seau!*' rang out, as someone filled their bucket and needed an empty one. Every now and again a clandestine grape found its way into your mouth (don't tell Antoine). Every now and again you'd look up and catch a rueful grin from your opposite number. It made it all seem worth while.

At last we were done. Twenty-three rows and 2.5 tonnes of merlot grapes – not bad for a small band of largely inexperienced pickers. The patron was happy. The *cave* seemed to be happy. We were happy. It was over.

The traditional end to the *vendange*, at least *chez* Antoine, is the *grillade*. The chef from the local café appears and, over a fire lit in a circle of stones, produces brochettes and steaks and baked potatoes, with home-made *pâté* to start and home-made apple pie to finish. And of course someone has brought along a guitar…

As the wine flowed and the stories got taller, we stretched our weary limbs and reflected fondly on the hot shower to come and a lie-in the next day.

And then it dawned on me. We hadn't done the *vendange* at all. True, our backs were broken, our fingers cut to ribbons, the nails stained purple in perpetuity. True, a tolerant friend had allowed us to bumble round his vineyard for a day, and we had hopefully repaid him for the experience by picking a useful amount of grapes. But that's not the REAL *vendange*.

The real *vendange* is done, increasingly these days, by machine, or if by hand then by gangs of hardy annuals who arrive for the season and pick doggedly day after day. The men and women who answer ads like the one in our local bar: 'Grape pickers needed at Roquessels. Three weeks' work'. Three *weeks*? I couldn't manage three days.

But next year, I thought to myself. Well maybe, just maybe…

FOUR:
Endings

I'm a Londoner. I am. I own an Oyster card, for goodness' sake. I Mind the Gap. On the underground platform, if someone tries to get ahead of me in the race for the opening doors, I cut smoothly across her bows, never by the twitch of an eyelid even acknowledging that she is there. Once on the Tube, I can read the next man's Metro upside-down and back to front quicker than you can say Banner Headlines.

London through and through, like a stick of Hackney rock.

Dark days

From: patrick@thestonehouse.fr
Sent   june 18 2008
To: nick@stoner.co.uk
Subject: news of a sort

Hi bro

Sorry it's been a while, but things got a bit weird round here and although it's all sorted now, we've been adjusting.

Last time we spoke I mentioned I hadn't been feeling too good. I couldn't really describe what was wrong, but I just didn't feel right. Eventually I got nagged into visiting the new German doctor and he couldn't find anything obvious and started asking questions about past lifestyle and drug usage. During which he took some blood samples and muttered about hepatitis.

Anyway, just over a week ago, Thursday night, he phoned. He'd just got the results from a blood test and he told me to stop drinking. Not cut down a bit. Stop. And that night. There's a liver test, gamma test I think,

162

anyway, it was supposed to be between 5 and 80 and mine was 2700. No, I didn't stick in an extra nought. My response was to get well-pissed, which was bloody stupid, I know.

After a bit of a sleepless night I went down to his surgery and he told me that I had six months. None of this bandying about the niceties. Straight-in. Six months and I'm dead. If, and it was an if, I stayed off it I might get a bit longer.

The last couple of weeks have not been good. The gamma test went up to 2800. The lab reckoned most people died before 2000. But he's been taking blood which makes my blood regenerate more red or white cells. Whichever. And the gamma is starting to drop. Meaning there might be a chance.

I'm a bit shell-shocked. It's been a massive change in my lifestyle, if that's the right word. I don't know right now what the long term is going to be, but I am worried about Patricia. Who is being bloody magnificent while I'm wallowing around in self-pity. As now.

So, I will write again shortly, when we know what's going on.

Love to you and the family
P

* * * * * *

We'd been in denial, but now we had to face the facts: Himself had succumbed to the ex-pat's disease. Too much leisure, too many parties, too many convivial get-togethers in the bar – it creeps up on you. We were soon to discover he was not alone: our wonderful new German doctor, who spoke excellent, crisp and Germanic English, took no prisoners.

Two others among our circle were seen to emerge from the surgery looking pale, clutching print-outs from the Clinique Pasteur laboratory in sweaty hands. Suddenly talk in the bar switched from who was sleeping with whom to who had the highest gamma levels. Jean-Paul laid in an extra stock of Perrier and did a roaring trade in non-alcoholic beer, which some wag immediately christened '*sans plomb*' (unleaded).

As for Himself, a strong constitution, a fairly healthy diet and the fact that he had given up smoking some ten years earlier somehow, miraculously, pulled him through. But it was a serious wake-up call which he was sensible enough to heed.

Life took a turn for the better, and the worse. On the plus side, our social life widened out: we could go to lunch and even dinner without having to drive home down the back roads with a drop taken so as to avoid the increasingly vigilant *gendarmes*. On the other hand, as Himself discovered, those long, intense, profoundly wise discussions in the bar that went on long into the night were suddenly seen to be neither wise nor profound without the lubrication of alcohol. 'I'd no idea just how *boring* those people were,' he declared to me wide-eyed after a particularly protracted and abstemious session.

Biting back a wifely 'I've been telling you that for years,' I smiled. 'Yes, dear,' I said.

Dark nights

While Himself was battling his demons, I was beginning to have a few of my own to contend with.

It was autumn again. When we first bought the Morbignan house the autumns were long and golden. We enjoyed the cooler weather: once again we could lunch on the terrace, no longer an inferno at noon. Once again our little river would flow chuckling over the stepping stones; the song of happy frogs would replace the scratching call of the crickets in the vines.

The long evenings when we sat on into the dusk until nearly midnight were behind us, but winter promised only crisp days and bright sunlight.

We had made many Christmas visits to the house, shivering deliciously in the odd cold snap and roasting chestnuts on the open fire, but we hadn't really experienced a full 21st Century Morbignan winter. In those early days we could rely on blindingly blue skies and temperatures which were brisk rather than chill. On one memorable occasion we went out with some friends for lunch on New Year's Day and actually got sunburned.

Bit by bit, though, things changed. Call it global warming or what you will, but the autumns got rainier and the winters danker and our Christmas visits became fewer and further between.

Then Purdey joined the family. Now the fleeting Christmas visits were made west, not east across the Channel; for the rest of the time, for better or worse, we were *Morbignanglais*.

There were compensations of course. Simon, our village mover and shaker, always had some project on the go. One year he had the bright idea of having a Halloween party. We would all dress up as monsters and ghouls and café-owner Jean Paul would lay on a suitably spooky feast. Even our French neighbours were enthused by the idea. Tiphaine the *antiquaire* conjured up a tall, pointy hat; Josiane carved a pumpkin lantern; P'tit Gui the builder found a crone's mask, some red and white striped stockings and a pair of high-heeled boots in which he wobbled around, cackling in our faces.

Not to be outdone, our English neighbours Penny and Robert came along in full fig as the Addams family. Penny had acquired a long black wig to cover her blonde curls and a long black dress to cling to her ample curves. Being a make-up artist by profession, she had done a wonderful job of turning the unkempt Robert into the smooth Gomez. With his hair oiled and slicked back and a pencil moustache, most of us didn't recognise him.

I had a plan. Scouring Komako I found a full-head skull mask with matching skeleton gloves. Patrick fashioned a scythe out of cardboard and a lot of tin foil. Clad in black jeans, high boots and a black hoodie top I would lurk in the car park until the guests – Himself and Purdey included - were assembled.

When the moment came to make my entrance, the reaction was all I could have wished. What was this vision of death, they all wondered, that came striding into the café flourishing its scythe, pointing a skeletal finger at this partygoer and that?

Alas, not everyone was taken in. As I made my way round the room trailing fear and giggles in my wake, something brushed against my booted calf. Something warm and furry. I looked down. Two bright brown eyes looked up at me. 'Oh,' said the assembled guests in disappointment. 'It's only Patricia.'

Then there was the day it snowed.

There is one thing that the French love even more than pronouncing the blindingly obvious, and that is telling you how to do things which, as a poor benighted Englishperson, you couldn't possibly be expected to manage on your own.

It was New Year's Eve, as it happens. We had been invited to a party by some friends whose house boasts a magnificent vaulted *salon*. Unfortunately this *salon* is so huge that in winter no amount of log fires, gas heaters and radiators can make an impression on the tomb-like cold which inhabits the room. I seriously do not do cold, and I was not looking forward to the party.

The snow started at around midday. Snow in our parts is not unheard-of, but it is rare. And snow that sticks and settles and can actually be crunched underfoot is a phenomenon to be regarded with respect. At least, that is, by the locals. And so it was that, as we later learned, the polite regrets started to flood in. By the time party time arrived, the gathering - now greatly lessened in numbers and mercifully to be held in the much warmer kitchen - was reduced to a handful of stalwart British, who had actually travelled to get there, plus a few French people who lived virtually next door.

Now in those days Himself boasted a very large Land Rover. It was his pride and joy. It could off-road with the best of them, and even though it had never actually been further than Spain, it could do the Paris-Dakar rally if asked. 'Snow?' said Himself and the beast collectively. 'Pshaw!'

But the French were seriously worried. Would we be able to get home, they wondered. Would we survive these terrifying conditions? And then, inevitably, came the pronouncement. 'You must let your tyres down,' they told him. 'It's the only thing to do.'

Patrick does not take kindly to being told what to do. Especially where his Land Rover is concerned. He was polite, in a gritted-teeth kind of way, but needless to say he did not let his tyres down. And when we had negotiated the half-mile or so home and were safely indoors again, he voiced his main grievance. 'I wouldn't mind so much,' he complained, 'but what on earth do *they* know about driving on snow?'

Unfortunately these incidents were bright spots in an otherwise increasingly bleak experience. Winters in Morbignan were becoming more and more of a trial, and my thoughts began to stray.

The final straw came the day we returned from a Christmas visit to London. The flat had been warm and welcoming, and after we had removed some six months' worth of dust, changed a couple of lightbulbs, put up the Christmas cards and hung some tinsel it was positively idyllic. We partied long and hard with friends and relatives, and even Purdey put up with the confinement for the sake of extra cuddles – and a few clandestine tit-bits.

After two weeks, though, the lure of Morbignan began to make itself felt. Ever the optimists, we remembered only the bright winter days, the walks in the pine wood, the cosy evenings round the open fire. We'd taken our precautions, of course. Throwing thrift to the winds we had switched on our newly-installed and eye-wateringly expensive central heating; the thermostat was turned to 10 degrees to prevent any freezing of pipes, but our neighbour was on standby to turn it up to a comfortable 20 degrees ahead of our return. The same neighbour volunteered to get in some shopping for us, so we were all set.

Nobody told us the flu had struck in Morbignan. We alerted Penny by email that we'd be arriving on December 27th, and she emailed back that all was well. We heard nothing more.

On a freezing night just before New Year's Eve we arrived, thankfully, at the little street which ran at the base of our kitchen steps. We were tired – the journey had been long and fraught. We were hungry – the restaurants in the last two *aires* we tried had been shut tight for the holidays. And while we weren't exactly cold – even a Land rover has a functioning heater these days – we could *see* the cold, pressing against the windows. We couldn't wait to get indoors.

The cold in the kitchen struck us like a fist. Obviously something had gone badly wrong: the radiators leaked a timid warmth that barely indented the chill – the thermostat had not been turned up. We could, and did, turn it up at once, but bitter experience had taught us that it took at least a day for the radiators to do their job and the house to achieve some semblance of warmth. Never mind, said Himself cheerfully, we'll light a fire. Small snag: there was no firewood – we had been intending to buy a *stère* or two from our friendly village woodsman when we got back to Morbignan after the holidays.

Never mind, said Himself cheerfully, we'll light the gas heaters. Ah. We'd been meaning to lay in gas before we left for England, but...

Never mind, said I cheerfully, a bowl of soup will warm us up nicely. The cupboard was bare.

We looked at each other. There was only one thing for it. Re-donning the boots and warm jackets we had just shed, we headed for the bar. It was shut.

169

That night we got into bed fully-clothed, puffer jackets and all, with the dog between us, and all three of us shivered the hours away. It was not an auspicious return.

Of course, a lot of this was our fault: the lack of food, gas and firewood - you couldn't blame the house for that. And no-one could foresee the fact that Penny and her husband would be laid low the day before our arrival with a particularly nasty bout of flu. You couldn't blame the house for that either. But somehow it got me thinking.

Then a chance encounter sealed the matter.

A radical re-think: the tiresome foreigner

We'd had three weeks of almost unremitting rain when the phone call came. My heart sank when I heard the voice: it was my most demanding client. He had a problem that only my presence in London could fix.   Most of my work by then involved writing, which I could happily do while holed up in Morbignan, a glass of wine at my elbow and Purdey warming my feet. Copy and images flew back and forth across the ether and press releases could just as easily be emailed from France as from England. Friends working in the UK were green with envy: I had, they grumbled, got it made.

Not this time, unfortunately. Now there was a press launch in the offing and, failing a sophisticated hologram, my actual physical presence was required. Then it struck me: London. Bright lights, shops, theatres. Friends I hadn't seen in ages. A warm flat. Suddenly the idea of going back didn't seem so bad after all.

It didn't take too long to take care of business, then I was free to enjoy myself back in the city which a small part of me still thought of as home. Morbignan, I mused, was at its best in summer: cool morning walks along the river bank, leisurely lunches on the shady terraces of cafes while the midday sun baked the earth to a red brown; a glass of *Picpoul de Pinet* with friends as the blue dusk settled on another scented evening.

And then it happened. There I was, striding out along High Holborn when up by my elbow popped the inevitable Tiresome Foreigner. Could I, he bleated above the roar of a departing bus, direct him to Hatton Garden? 'So sorry,' I trilled sweetly. 'Afraid I don't know. You see, I don't live here.'

The lie came smoothly to my lips, I thought, feeling rather pleased with myself. That got rid of him. Then I stopped dead in my tracks, frozen with horror. It was true. What I had just said was literally... true.

I'm a Londoner. I am. According to my mother, Gertrude Shilling's son David (the milliner) was born in the same Welbeck Street clinic as I. How London is that? I own an Oyster card, for goodness' sake. I Mind the Gap. On the underground platform, if someone tries to get ahead of me in the race for the opening doors, I cut smoothly across her bows, never by the twitch of an eyelid even acknowledging that she is there. Once on the Tube, I can read the next man's Metro upside-down and back to front quicker than you can say Banner Headlines. I'm London through and through, like a stick of Hackney rock.

But I didn't live in London any more. I wasn't a Londoner: I was a *Morbignanglais*. And for the first time the idea depressed me.

The whole thing had crept up on me with sneaky footsteps. An extra week in France? An extra month? Just a nice long stay in my holiday home, I told my envious friends. 'Oh, I could never be a year-rounder' I would boast to France-based ex-pat friends. Then a pair of brown eyes and a stumpy tail came into the equation and everything changed. I turned, without a backward glance, from a sleek city rat into a humble country mouse. A French country mouse. And suddenly this would not do at all.

I returned to France with a smile on my face and determination in my heart. By hook or by crook, we were going home.

House hunting... again

Months of negotiation followed. My husband did not like London. My dog emphatically did not like London. It seemed I was outnumbered. Then inspiration struck.

First of all, I slyly used language as a sweetener. Wouldn't Himself just love to be able to chat about his beloved Land Rover in English again? Most of his 4x4-minded mates were French, with as little grasp of our language as Himself had of theirs.

And, I added, remember how you get so bored in the bar, when everyone has a drop taken and is talking rubbish, and you sitting boot-faced over a glass of *sans-plomb*? Wouldn't you like to be able to choose your friends because of shared interests, rather than a shared language?

Next I appealed to comfort, of which Himself is extremely fond. We'd had several winters of rain and cold and howling winds - and our house was not built with cold and wet in mind. Tiled floors downstairs and wooden ones above are not exactly cosy when the wind keens in the rooftops. Yes, we could make the salon snug with a crackling, sweet-smelling log fire, boosted discreetly by a gas heater. Yes, a cold bedroom and warm duvets were delicious, especially with the addition of a remote-controlled electric heater to take the morning chill off the room before we got up. But venture to the loo, go into the kitchen to put the kettle on, and you returned blue and shivering.

Regular use of our central heating was out of the question. We had the radiators, but no town gas, so that we were reliant on large and extremely expensive cylinders delivered fortnightly from the local depot. Their contents disappeared at an alarming rate without making much impression on the cold indoors.

'Carpets,' I coaxed Himself. '*Real* central heating...'

Then I produced my ace. How would it be, I asked husband and dog, if I could find a compromise? Somewhere within striking distance of London, to feed my addiction? Somewhere green enough to enjoy the benefits of rural life, including nice long walks which didn't involve pavements? Somewhere as friendly as our village in France, but where chatting over the purchase of a dozen eggs could be conducted in English?

After all, I pleaded sweetly, we would still have France. We would still spend long, long holidays there. We would have the luxury of complaining about the heat, safe in the knowledge that at the first hint of autumnal gales we would be off to more comfortable surroundings. Slowly I won them round. It was time to go house-hunting again.

Just as in those far-off, heady days when we trudged the streets of St Rémy with Jean-Jacques, we had a shopping list. A garden was a *sine qua non*. Never mind that I knew absolutely nothing about gardening; never mind that every plant I had ever owned turned black and died within days. A garden we had to have, if only to avoid the late-night dog walks round the neighbourhood streets.

Then there was a garage. Patrick is partial to garages. Not that any car he has ever owned will actually fit in a garage: the doorway to the one we had in Morbignan was too low, and besides the street was so narrow it was impossible to manoeuvre the Land Rover into it. However, a garage comes in useful for lots of things – most of them junk, I reminded him bitterly, but still…

Easy access to London was a deal-breaker. Friends, theatres, even the occasional client resided in London, and on that point I was firm. We considered the Midlands. We considered Cornwall. We even considered East Anglia, until our good friends from Ipswich pointed out the drawbacks of the wind (fierce) and the rail service (practically non-existent).

In the end, of course, it was a no-brainer. Himself was born in Sussex. Many a time during our life in London he had remarked, wistfully, that one day he'd like to go and live beside the sea. I scoffed mightily. What, retire to the seaside? What a cliché. Just when you're getting old and set in your ways you up-sticks from everything and everyone you know and go and live in some remote resort which is dead in the winter and teeming with grockles in the summer. What genius thought that one up?

Now it was his turn to win me round. It happened that we were going to England as a family to catch up with some old friends of Himself's, and he found us a holiday cottage in West Sussex - just for a week, of course. It was February. It was cold and wet and windy. The house, on the other hand, was snug and welcoming. It was also three minutes' walk from the beach. Purdey was ecstatic. Even through the rain I could see it was a beautiful beach, with a wide swathe of green above it that stretched for two miles or more. The rare dog-walkers we passed raised rain-sodden faces and smiled hello. After two days of this I capitulated. 'It wouldn't be so bad to live here,' I remarked.

Back in Morbignan we began to make plans. Patrick had cunningly secured a street map of the little town where we had stayed, and we pored over it. 'Near the beach,' begged Purdey. 'Near the shops,' I insisted. Eventually we selected the ideal location, half way between the beach and the High Street. And, in the teeth of all improbability, this is where we found our new English home.

And so it was that on a November day in 2011 we were on the road again, heading north. Away from the vines and the olives and the *petit pastis* at 6 o'clock in the village bar. Back to the land where, my French friends assured me, it rains or snows or is foggy 365 days a year.

But not forever. After almost a quarter of a century, the Languedoc is in our blood. We shall return. There will always come the moment: every year, like restless swallows, we will know when it's time to fly south.

Time to meet the friends who will greet us like long-lost dear ones (the friends who have scarcely noticed our absence). Time to renew acquaintance with the good ol' boys in the square and marvel at all the new things Jean-Paul has done with the bar (there won't be much). Time to remember how much we love the early summer mornings when the promise of heat hangs heavy over the hills; the lazy siestas, the gatherings round barbecues and – yes! – the *petit pastis* at 6 o'clock.

After all, we will always be at home in the Pays d'Oc.

< the end >

ACKNOWLEDGEMENTS

I would like to thank all the friends, neighbours, acquaintances and customs officials who, wittingly or unwittingly, provided material for this book.

At Home in the Pays d'Oc is loosely based on real people and real events. I have changed names and done my best not to offend anyone, and in this I hope I have succeeded.

However, should anyone ever come up to me and say: 'It didn't happen like that,' I can only reply in the words of an old news editor I knew many years ago: 'Never spoil a good story for the sake of a few facts.'

PAW PRINTS IN THE BUTTER
Patricia Feinberg Stoner
With illustrations by Bob Bond

Are there paw prints in the butter?
Is there a nose mark on the pane?
Is there fluff beneath the sofa?
THAT CAT's been here again.

In this clowder of cats curious and comical, you will
 * Meet Lulu the Terrible and find out how she fell from grace…
 * Shudder at the menace of The Cat Who Howls in the Night and laugh with the irrepressible Stationery Cat…
 * Learn how the ancient Cabriole won his lady love, and how she rewarded him…
 * And listen, with the wide-eyed kitten, to the mewmoirs of The Cat Who Has Been Here Before.

'If you have a cat, know a cat, or have ever interacted with a cat, this collection of poems will have you chuckling, or at least smiling knowingly' - Ingénue Magazine

Manufactured by Amazon.com
Columbia, SC
11 April 2017